The New Americans
Recent Immigration and American Society

Edited by
Steven J. Gold and Rubén G. Rumbaut

A Series from LFB Scholarly

Recruiting Hispanic Labor
Immigrants in Non-Traditional Areas

Karen D. Johnson-Webb

LFB Scholarly Publishing LLC
New York 2003

Copyright © 2003 by LFB Scholarly Publishing LLC

All rights reserved.

Library of Congress Cataloging-in-Publication Data

Johnson-Webb, Karen D.
  Recruiting Hispanic labor : immigrants in non-traditional areas / Karen D. Johnson-Webb.
     p. cm. -- (The new Americans : recent immigration and American society)
  Includes bibliographical references.
  ISBN 1-931202-66-4 (alk. paper)
  1. Alien labor, Latin American--Recruiting--North Carolina--Research Triangle Park Region. 2. Alien labor, Spanish--Recruiting--North Carolina--Research Triangle Park Region. 3. United States—Emigration and immigration. 4. Latin America--Emigration and immigration. 5. Spain--Emigration and immigration. I. Title: Immigrants in non-traditional areas. II. Title. III. New Americans (LFB Scholarly Publishing LLC).
  HD8081.H7J64 2003
  331.6'2807565--dc21

2003003571

ISBN 1-931202-66-4

Printed on acid-free 250-year-life paper.

Manufactured in the United States of America.

TABLE OF CONTENTS

ACKNOWLEDGEMENTS vii
CHAPTER 1 1
  Migration Research in Geography 1
    Introduction 1
    Definition of Terms 4
    Limitations of the Study 6
CHAPTER 2 7
  Migration Theory, Immigration Policy and Demographic Change 7
    Introduction 7
    Migration Theory 8
    U.S. Immigration Policy 12
    Restructuring of the Economy 15
    Development of the Sunbelt 21
    Employer Attitudes and Perceptions 24
    Gaps in the Migration Theories 27
CHAPTER 3 31
  National Context of Hispanic Population Change 31
    Introduction 31
    Redistribution of the Hispanic Population 38
CHAPTER 4 39
  Midwest Context of Hispanic Population Change 39
    Introduction 39
    A Brief History 39
    Demographic Change in the Midwest 42
    Local Scale Demographic Change in the Midwest 45
CHAPTER 5 47
  North Carolina Context of Hispanic Population Change 47
    Introduction 47

Background and Present Context 47
Other Indicators of the Growing Presence of Hispanics
in North Carolina 56
Community Attitudes 62
CHAPTER 6 69
Research Methods 69
The Study Area 69
Data Collection Strategy and Methods 70
Newspaper Content Analysis 70
Key Informant Interviews 72
The Qualitative Corporate Interview 75
CHAPTER 7 79
Data Analysis and Results 79
Employer Preferences for Hispanic Labor 79
Formal Recruitment Strategies 84
Employment Intermediaries 94
Informal Methods of Recruitment 98
Accommodation Strategies 102
CHAPTER 8 113
Discussion and Conclusions 113
Discussion 113
Conclusions 116
Policy Implications of the Research Findings 117
Future Research 119
APPENDICES 121
A. North Carolina Counties 121
B. Photocopies of Original Help Wanted Advertisements
.... 122
NOTES 123
WORKS CITED 125
INDEX 147

ACKNOWLEDGEMENTS

This book is the culmination of several years work, however it was not completed without the help and guidance of several people and institutions. The faculty and support staff in the Department of Geography at the University of North Carolina at Chapel were indispensable in terms of institutional and moral support. Leo Zonn, and Steve Birdsall helped to shape this research in a myriad of ways. The North Carolina Rural Health and Policy Analysis Program at the Cecil G. Sheps Center for Health Services Research at the University of North Carolina also gave much technical and professional support as well. Dr. Thomas Ricketts was always willing to give any support he could along with his staff at the Sheps Center. Grants and fellowships supported this work, namely from the Center for Urban And Regional Studies (Charles and Shirley Weiss Fellowship); and from the Graduate School (Merit Fellowship); and the Department of Geography at UNC-Chapel Hill. The faculty at the Center for Policy Analysis & Public Service contributed advice and assistance, as did the Department of Geography Department at Bowling Green State University. It was James H. Johnson, however, who was instrumental in the shaping of this research project and provided the excellent mentorship that eventually made it a scholarly success. I would also like to acknowledge and thank those who participated in this research. It was their insights that were most important. And finally, I thank my family for their support and patience.

CHAPTER 1
Migration Research in Geography

Introduction

Immigrant labor migration has been an issue that has long been the subject of research by geographers and other social scientists. Ravenstein first published his theory of migration in the Geographical Magazine in 1876, and subsequently in the academic literature (Ravenstein 1885; Ravenstein 1889). In his view, the largest migration streams were generated "from the desire inherent in most men to 'better' themselves in material respects" (1889, p. 304). Since that time researchers have characterized major world migrations first and foremost as labor migrations (Portes 1978; Piore 1979; Salt 1989; Wilson 1993; Waldrauch 1995; Vargas 1999). More recently, migration theory has "placed" labor migrants within the international economic system that generates economic forces between geographical regions within that system. One example of one of these forces is the penetration of U.S. capital into other regions of the world, most notably, Mexico.

Geographers are particularly well suited for studying labor migration because they recognize and are experienced at studying problems at different scales and they recognize that scale is an important variable in any research problem. Geographers also tend use multi-disciplinary methods in their research. In addition to studying aspects of the actual movement of individuals and groups from one place to another, they are adept at focusing on smaller scale issues of this phenomenon.

The discipline of geography has a rich tradition of research on migration. Major contributions include the introduction of the concept of place utility and the primacy of migrants as actors in the process of migration (Wolpert 1965). Zelinsky's "mobility transition" influenced migration theory by shedding light on the changes that occur in population mobility during the process of modernization (Zelinsky 1971). Roseman developed a typology of migration, highlighting both the scale and temporal aspects of migration (Roseman 1971). Salt (1989), in his international overview of migration systems, identified several trends that were characteristic of these streams.

Geographers have also done empirical work in migration research. Internal redistribution of the U.S. population, including return migration to the South, has been studied extensively (Roseman 1977; McHugh 1987; Cromartie and Stack 1989; McHugh 1989; Johnson and Roseman 1990; Johnson and Grant 1997; Lee and Roseman 1997; Roseman and Lee 1998; Newbold 1999; Newbold and Spindler 2001). Berry and Dahmann were among the first researchers to describe the pattern of internal population redistribution that came to be known as the counterurbanization of the 1970s (Berry and Dahmann 1977). Geographers have also focused their research on the demographic characteristics of migrants as these relate to migration (Jones 1982; Plane and Isserman 1983; Jones 1984; Walker, Ellis et al. 1992; Johnson-Webb and Johnson 1996; Johnson, Johnson-Webb et al. 1999).

Large scale, long term trends in world migrations have also been studied (Berry 1993). Refugees and asylees (Desbarats 1985; Miyares 1997), settlement patterns of U.S. immigrants at various spatial scales (Boswell 1984; Dagodag 1984; Valdez and Jones 1984; Johnson, Johnson-Webb et al. 1999), and undocumented workers have been subjects of geographical research (Jones 1982; Dagodag 1984; Jones 1984; Cherry 1995).

The impact of immigrants on U.S. society, in terms of both microeconomic and macroeconomic explanations has become an important area of study that stems from the intense current popular and political (and security) interest in the issue. Assimilation and incorporation (Miyares 1997; Newbold 2000), heterolocalism (Zelinsky and Lee 1998), fiscal and economic impacts (Johnson and Oliver 1989); and social impacts (Johnson and Farrell 1993; Johnson, Farrell et al. 1997; Li 1998) are but a few of the topics being studied.

Researchers within other disciplines have also done important work on all of the topics described above: measuring migration streams (Tienda 1983; Lieberson and Waters 1987; Long 1988; Frey, Liaw et al. 1995; Hirschman, Kasinitz et al. 1999), the study of how economic and immigration policy is linked to migration streams (Briggs 1984; Griffith 1990; Griffith and Runsten 1992; Baker 1997), the role of employers in labor migration [(Piore 1979; Massey, Arango et al. 1993; Massey, Arango et al. 1994), and assimilation, adaptation and incorporation (Waldinger 1993; Portes 1996; Alba, Logan et al. 2000).

This research explores geographical aspects of the changes that are occurring in the internal distribution of the foreign-born Hispanic population of the United States.1 These changes are occurring most notably within rural areas and small- to medium-size urban areas in the Great Plains and in the Southeast, far removed from the traditional port of entry metropolitan areas that have typified immigrant settlement patterns in the past (Howlett 1995; Ribadeneira 1996; Branson 1997; Hendee 1997). These new settlements of Hispanics have rapidly and dramatically changed these smaller communities. The changes occurring in these communities, and the forces underlying these changes, have begun to be systematically documented and researched (Stull, Broadway et al. 1995; Broadway 2000; Suro and Singer 2002).

The South and the Midwest are the two regions that are being literally transformed by Hispanic immigrants (and indeed immigrants in general) (MDC 2002). In the Midwest, Chicago has long been its immigration gateway. However, rural, formerly homogenous communities are now under tremendous demographic change. The current trends in Hispanic population change in the Midwest will be illustrated in this study.

In the South, the state of North Carolina is one of the non-traditional locations that are experiencing a striking change in ethnic makeup. The Hispanic population growth in the South has been so dramatic that in recent research, the Raleigh-Durham-Chapel Hill Metropolitan Statistical Area was categorized as a "hyper-change" Latino area (Suro and Singer 2002). Since 1990, North Carolina's population has been transformed from one that was primarily White and Black, with a small but significant American Indian population. North Carolina now has the largest permanently settled Hispanic population in its history. Whereas North Carolina has had a significant Hispanic migrant farm worker population for several decades, what is new about this latest influx of Hispanics is their settlement in urban areas and their engagement in primarily non-agricultural work.

The central purpose of this research was to examine the recent immigration and in-migration of Hispanic immigrants to areas of the United States that have not historically experienced immigration. The role of formal and informal labor recruitment strategies utilized by North Carolina employers were assessed. Further, this research determined whether employers in North Carolina recruited immigrant Hispanic workers to urban areas, as well as the methods and mechanisms they used to recruit them.

This research is significant in several ways. First, it adds to the body of knowledge about the internal redistribution of the Hispanic population in the U.S. It links international migration to North Carolina with social, economic, and political change and aids in understanding the causes of the rapid demographic changes occurring in North Carolina and how these are spatially distributed. In other words, this study explores the phenomenon of Hispanic migration to North Carolina in its wider social, demographic, economic and political context.

Second, the recent influx of Hispanics into North Carolina's urban areas is a dramatic demographic change, and one that has far-reaching economic, social and political implications. The large increase of Hispanic immigrants into non-traditional areas has ramifications for the social fabric of these communities. This study will inform immigration policy more generally and local social policy specifically. It is a foundation for future research in that, these same types of questions, and some of the answers revealed here, can be used as a basis for research of this type in other Southeastern and Midwestern communities.

Finally, the role that employers play in this mass immigration to North Carolina and indeed to the U.S. is explored in depth in this research. This question has received little attention in the past. Employer preferences and recruiting behavior may be a major factor driving immigration to North Carolina from Mexico, and if this is true, immigration policy must address this issue.

Definition of Terms

The following section is a glossary of terms that will be used throughout the study.

Immigration- the process of entering and settling in a land to which one is not native.

Migration- the process of moving from one region or state within a particular country and settling in another region or state within that country.

In-migration- the process of entering a region and settling there.
Recruitment strategies- plans or methods that employers use in order to recruit workers.

Employment intermediaries- individuals or agencies that act as agents between employers and prospective employees.

Hispanics- those who classified themselves in one of the specific Hispanic origin categories listed in the U.S. Census questionnaire-- "Mexican," "Puerto Rican," "Cuban," "Dominican"--as well as those who indicated that they were of the Spanish-speaking countries of Central America or South America. Persons of "Other Spanish/Hispanic" origin are those who came from Spain, or they are persons of Hispanic origin identifying themselves generally as Spanish, Spanish-American, Hispanic, Hispano, Latino, and so forth (U.S. Department of Commerce, 1993).

Native-born workers- those that were born in the U.S.

In-migration Field- the overall spatial pattern of migration flows to a specific metropolitan area (Roseman & McHugh, 1982).

Industry Sector- a specific branch of manufacturing and trade, e.g. retail or manufacturing.

PUMA- Public Use Microdata Area. A geographic area created for the 1990 Public Use Microdata Samples (PUMS). These areas replace the "county groups" used in the 1980 PUMS files and were defined by each state or local area according to the Census Bureau specifications. Each PUMA must have at least 100,000 population and consists of a whole county or a subcounty area such as a minor civil division (MCD) in New England, a place, or a group of tracts. Counties or subcounty areas less than 100,000 were combined to produce PUMAs of at least 100,000 population. In the 1990 PUMS files, PUMAs are used to define (1) current residence in 1990, (2) residence in 1985, and (3) place of work (U.S. Bureau of Census 1993).

PUMS- Public Use Microdata 5% Sample. Computerized files containing a sample of individual long-form decennial census records containing most population and housing characteristics (U.S. Bureau of Census 1993).

H-2A visa- issued by the Immigration and Naturalization Service (INS) to temporary or seasonal agricultural workers where U.S. agricultural workers are unavailable. This visa is issued for one year with two one-year extensions allowed. Employers must demonstrate a need for workers in this category (ASN American Services Network 1998).

H-2B visa- issued by the INS to temporary workers coming to the U.S. to engage in non-agricultural employment which is seasonal, intermittent, to meet peak load need, or for a one-time occurrence where U.S. workers are unavailable. This visa is issued for one year with two one-year extensions allowed. Employers must demonstrate a need for workers in this category (ASN, American Services Network 1998).

Limitations of the Study

There are several limitations of the study. First, the research on employer recruitment is focused on one state, North Carolina, and on a qualitative sample of employers, therefore the results of this study cannot be generalized to other states. Second, the push factors in sending regions or communities of origin were not dealt with in any detail in this study. This aspect of the Hispanic immigration to the U.S., although not within the scope of this study, is one that must be acknowledged and considered in order to provide a truly contextual explanation. Third, Hispanic workers were not interviewed for this study and hence, a very important perspective is missing.

CHAPTER 2
Migration Theory, Immigration Policy and Demographic Change

Introduction

The vast majority of immigrants who come to the U.S. do so primarily in search of employment. Since the beginnings of mass migration to the U.S., employers or their agents have recruited foreign labor through various means (McWilliams, 1948; Portes, 1985; Vargas, 1999). Recent accounts also exist which suggest or document that U.S. employers actively engage in recruiting immigrant labor (Griffith, 1993; Cherry, 1995; Hedges, 1996; Johnson-Webb 2002).

Recruiting of immigrant labor by employers is a crucial factor in the process of labor migration, but it cannot fully explain the recent appearance of Hispanics, especially families, in North Carolina's urban areas. Many factors have contributed to the dramatic demographic changes occurring in North Carolina and the Southeastern U.S. These factors include immigration policy since 1965, the restructuring of the economy and the increased globalization of industry, which accelerated in the 1970s and 1980s. Major demographic trends in the U.S. also played a role. These factors can be described or categorized in terms of changes in the supply of and demand for labor in the South. Figure 2.1 is a schema of the theoretical framework for this study. It illustrates the interaction between demand side and supply side factors and recent U.S. immigration policy, as well as changes in the global economy and how these interactions have been manifested at the national, regional, and local scales in the U.S.

Figure 2-1 Conceptual and Theoretical Framework

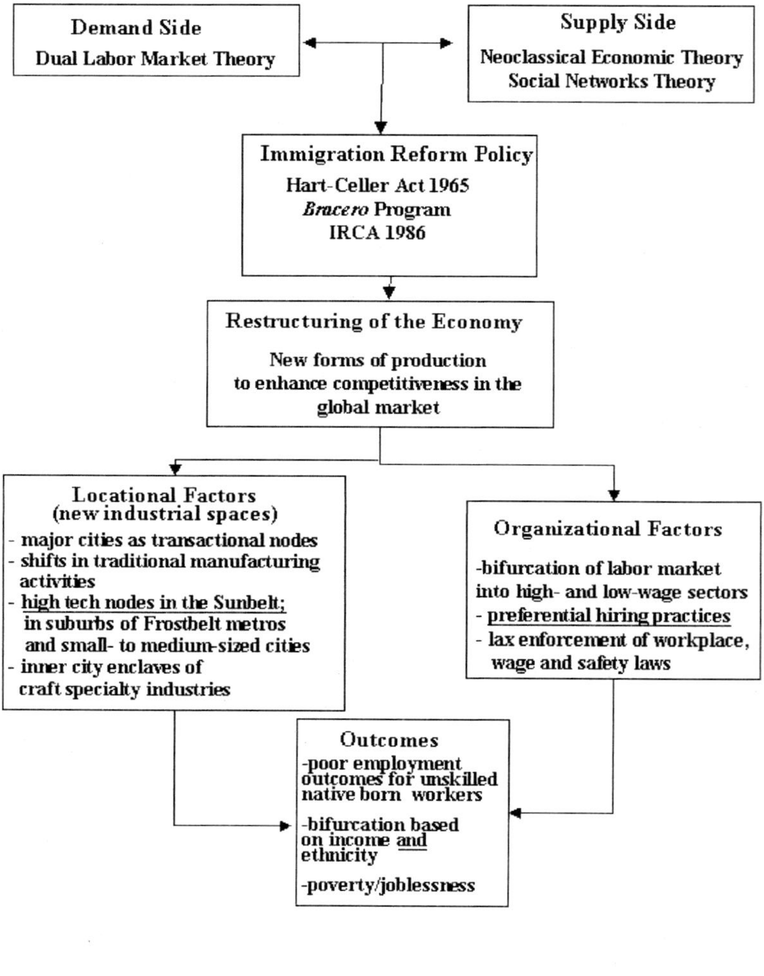

```
┌─────────────────────────┐         ┌─────────────────────────────┐
│      Demand Side        │◄───────►│        Supply Side          │
│ Dual Labor Market Theory│         │ Neoclassical Economic Theory│
│                         │         │   Social Networks Theory    │
└─────────────────────────┘         └─────────────────────────────┘
              │
              ▼
        ┌──────────────────────────┐
        │ Immigration Reform Policy│
        │    Hart-Celler Act 1965  │
        │       Bracero Program    │
        │         IRCA 1986        │
        └──────────────────────────┘
                    │
                    ▼
        ┌──────────────────────────┐
        │ Restructuring of the Economy │
        │   New forms of production    │
        │ to enhance competitiveness in│
        │       the global market      │
        └──────────────────────────┘
             │                    │
             ▼                    ▼
┌──────────────────────────┐  ┌──────────────────────────┐
│    Locational Factors    │  │  Organizational Factors  │
│ (new industrial spaces)  │  │                          │
│ - major cities as        │  │ -bifurcation of labor    │
│   transactional nodes    │  │  market into high- and   │
│ - shifts in traditional  │  │  low-wage sectors        │
│   manufacturing activities│  │ - preferential hiring    │
│ - high tech nodes in the │  │   practices              │
│   Sunbelt; in suburbs of │  │ - lax enforcement of     │
│   Frostbelt metros and   │  │   workplace, wage and    │
│   small- to medium-sized │  │   safety laws            │
│   cities                 │  │                          │
│ - inner city enclaves of │  │                          │
│   craft specialty industries│ │                        │
└──────────────────────────┘  └──────────────────────────┘
                  │               │
                  ▼               ▼
              ┌──────────────────────────┐
              │        Outcomes          │
              │ -poor employment outcomes│
              │  for unskilled native    │
              │  born workers            │
              │ -bifurcation based on    │
              │  income and ethnicity    │
              │ -poverty/joblessness     │
              └──────────────────────────┘
```

Migration Theory

Piore and others posit that the labor demands of modern industrial societies are the most important forces for migration (Piore 1979; Grosfoguel and CorderoGuzman 1998; Massey 1999; Arango 2000; Delechat 2001; Iredale 2001). This demand is fueled by the interactions between labor-surplus and labor scarce economies (Goss and Lindquist 1995). In capitalist societies, labor scarce labor markets are divided into two segments. The primary sector is characterized by well-paying jobs with secure tenure and fringe benefits. The secondary sector contains jobs that are low paying and menial (Piore 1979; Massey, Arango et al. 1993). Native-born workers are reluctant to work at jobs in the secondary sector; therefore, employers are always looking to recruit immigrant labor to fill them (Portes and Sensenbrenner 1993; Cornelius 1998).

Migration scholars have come to realize that much of the world's labor migrations have become a transnational process (Portes, 1996; Hirschman, Kasinitz et al., 1999; Rodriguez, 1999; Landolt Marticorena, 2000; Levitt, 2001). A migrant's stay is viewed as being of a temporary nature and migrants are perceived to have come to the receiving regions solely to reach an economic goal in terms of earnings. Migrants are also viewed as making and keeping strong connections between the communities of which they are a part, the home region and the receiving region. This view is in direct contradiction to conventional views of migration and immigration in which the return of the migrant is viewed as a failure to succeed on the part of the migrant. Within this context, the return of migrants to their home country can be viewed as a success, especially if they have met the economic goals they set for themselves. Conversely, migrants who find themselves "settling out" might be considered failed in their aspirations (Piore 1979).

Employer recruitment has been viewed by some as the most salient factor in migration (Piore, 1979). Once migration streams are started in this way, they are almost impossible to stem. Jobs in the receiving regions tend to be low-skilled, low paying, connote low social status and often involve hard or unpleasant working conditions (Cornelius 2000). Additionally, many of these jobs, to which immigrants are attracted, seldom offer advancement, are performed in unstructured work environments, and involve informal and extremely personalistic relationships between supervisors and subordinates. This type of work might have connotations in the migrants' home country, but because they are away from home, their status there is not affected. In fact, their social status is enhanced there by the relative material wealth they are able to confer upon their families in the home country.

There is overwhelming evidence of the importance of employer recruitment in various migrations of workers to the U.S. Before World War II, employers sent agents to Europe to recruit workers (Piore 1979; Portes and Bach 1985). Labor recruiters have also been sent to Mexico at various times, and agents of the steel mills, sugar beet industry and auto industry among others were instrumental in attracting rural labor from the South during the Great Migration (Cardenas 1978; Portes 1978). Dual labor market theory places the impetus for international immigration squarely on the shoulders of U.S. employers. Their need for labor and, as will be shown below, their desire for certain types of workers, is a strong pull factor for international migrants, especially those in developing countries.

Migration theory is also helpful in explaining the characteristics and size of the labor supply in the U.S. Neoclassical economic theory of migration focuses on the wage and employment differentials between sending and receiving countries (Massey 1999). Migrant streams of workers move from low-wage to high-wage countries. Subsequently, upward pressure is exerted on wages in sending regions and downward pressure on wages in receiving regions until equilibrium is reached. Markets are seen to be perfectly functioning, and decisions to migrate are portrayed as individual ones made to optimize earning potential through measuring costs and benefits. Ravenstein all but dismissed push factors such as oppression, taxation, and societal upheaval, in favor of personal gain (Ravenstein 1889; Lee 1966). Individual characteristics of immigrants are perceived to increase or decrease the likelihood that they will migrate, and international migration is believed to continue until the wage gap is closed (Zolberg 1989). Under this theoretical framework, immigrants would go to the country that would yield them the highest gain in wages, and settle there permanently.

The "new economics of migration" has basically moved this argument from the individual level to that of the family or household (Massey, Arango et al. 1993; Espenshade 1997). Instead of wage differentials being the main impetus for international migration, the failures of other markets (and not solely the labor market) threaten the economic well being of households in sending regions. These markets may be insurance markets or markets for capital, for example. Therefore, the "new economics" implicitly recognizes that markets are not perfectly functioning and that they may leave households open to the risk of losing their income, or property, or to the possibility of not being able to access scarce resources in their region of origin.

In order to insulate themselves from the risks imposed by malfunctioning markets, households often send one or more members abroad to work and earn wages. The "new economics of migration" views this as a means for households to "diversify their labor portfolios" (Massey et al, 1994, p. 712). Sending a family member to work abroad is viewed as a way to improve the family's economic status at home, through cash remittances. These remittances are used by households in the regions of origin for local investment and consumption. In neoclassical theory, international migration only affects the level of wages in sending regions. The "new economics" portrays sending communities as closely linked with national and international markets through the cash remittances sent by emigrant family members.

Neoclassical theory and the new economics of migration relate to the supply of labor in that they partially explain the decision to migrate by individuals. Those that opt to better themselves economically add to the supply of labor in the U.S., and if there were no migrants willing to move, there would be no voluntary migration regardless of the availability of employment or the recruitment efforts of employers in distant locations. The importance of remittances in the sending economy is an integral part of the migration process and is a major impetus for immigrant workers to come to the U.S. to earn relatively better wages.

World systems theory of migration and Sassen's global cities framework, which is closely linked with world systems theory, is helpful in explaining how certain localities could become hotbeds of immigration (Sassen 1991). Although this theory does not fully explain this phenomenon, certain aspects of it ring true. Massey (1993), Sassen, and others characterized migration within the world systems framework as a result of the expansion of the global economy into peripheral regions of the world (Sassen-Koob 1981; Sassen 1996). Within the context of world systems theory, immigration is said to be a natural outgrowth of the process of capitalist development and its disruptions and dislocations. Material and cultural links are generated between the developed and developing countries (as has been the case between the U.S. and Mexico and other parts of Central America). This is facilitated by consolidation of land, by extraction of raw materials, and exploitation of cheap labor in developing countries (Portes and Bach 1985; Zolberg 1989; Massey, Arango et al. 1994).

Once international migration is initiated, several forces may fuel its perpetuation. Local scale factors can influence the decision to migrate. Network theory of migration assumes a set of declining costs and declining risks that immigrants have to take due to social ties they can draw upon in the destination communities (Massey, Arango et al. 1993; Massey, Arango et al. 1994). These social ties constitute a form of social capital for immigrants. Studies have shown that the existence of migrant networks lowers the risks experienced or perceived by a potential immigrant (Walker and Hannan 1989). Immigrants who have the benefits of kinship ties with people who have already migrated to a receiving community are said to be more likely to migrate to that community. Institutional theory of migration broadens that of network theory. Institutions usually emerge in response to an influx of immigrants to these communities. These institutions assist immigrants in obtaining housing, education, health care, legal assistance, job placement, and perhaps even assist them in gaining residency or citizenship status. Communities that contain one or more of these institutions may be more attractive to immigrants and therefore help perpetuate migration streams to that community.

Because immigrant Hispanic agricultural workers have been present in the state since at least the early 1980s, social networks migration theory has implications for the supply of immigrant Hispanic labor on the local scale in North Carolina (Nelson 1990). Many of these agricultural workers were able to "settle out" of agricultural work after amnesty and gain more stable employment. Many of them began to bring their family members to North Carolina (Decierdo 1991; Bettez 1992; Levin, Rolon et al. 1995; Davis, Gildner et al. 1997). Additionally, as those who began to settle in North Carolina's urban communities told potential migrants in their communities of origin about job and housing opportunities, an informal network was developed which has become self-perpetuating as more immigrants come and bring more family members, and they tell other prospective immigrants about North Carolina.

U.S. Immigration Policy

Recent federal immigration policy has also contributed to the supply of immigrant labor. The policies of the U.S. government with respect to immigration have had an effect on the supply of immigrant labor in the U.S. both historically and in recent decades. From 1917 to 1922, the first *Bracero* Program was instituted due to pressure from agricultural interests in the southwestern U.S. (*Bracero* was corrupted from the Spanish word abrazo or arm). The *Bracero* program was created by separate Congressional enactments, not as a part of U.S. immigration policy. In 1942, the Mexican Farm Labor Program was instituted. It also took on the name "the *Bracero* Program." This program gave Mexican contract workers protection in terms of housing, transportation, food, medical needs, and wage rates. The program expired in 1947, but it was continued informally until 1951 (Briggs 1984; Briggs 1996; Baker 1997). After the Korean War in 1951, the program was extended on three different occasions until it was terminated in 1964. After the *Bracero* Program was terminated in 1964, undocumented immigration of agricultural workers began to accelerate, as the need for Mexicans to earn American wages and the demand of agricultural interests for cheap labor had not changed simply because the program had ended.

The Immigration and Reform Act of 1965 or the Hart-Celler Act, the precursor to "the new immigration," radically changed the size and makeup of the immigrant population in the United States (Briggs 1984; Bouvier and Gardner 1986; Waldinger 1989; Barkan 1990; Portes and Rumbaut 1996). This policy erased the racial quotas that for decades had restricted various non-European immigrants from emigrating to the U.S., most notably Asians.

The Hart-Celler Act was based on the principle of family reunification and removed restrictions on immigration based on race. Along with the massive dissemination of U.S. culture and capital, and political influence through the worldwide media, the new policy helped trigger, as well, a steady flow of immigration, both documented and undocumented from Latin America and Asia to the U.S. (Bean and Tienda 1987; Portes and Rumbaut 1996). Moreover. revolutionary upheavals in many Latin American and Asian countries, coupled with U.S. and Soviet military interventions abroad, resulted in a swelling refugee population in the U.S.

The most obvious consequence of the Immigration and Reform Act of 1965, and subsequent immigration legislation, was that it revived mass immigration to the U.S. It also resulted in a shift from western and Eastern Europe to Latin America and the Pacific Rim as the primary countries of origin for U.S. immigrants (Zolberg 1995; Briggs 1996; Johnson, Farrell et al. 1997). This mass infusion of immigrants has driven U.S. population growth in recent decades. The effects of this influx on the U.S. economy and the wages of the American labor force have been the focus of much research (Borjas 1990; Briggs 1996; Espenshade 1997). Also, by instituting numerical quotas on immigration and, therefore, creating excessively long backlogs for those trying to enter the country legally, the 1965 Act inadvertently triggered an explosion of undocumented immigration to the U.S.

The Immigration Reform and Control Act of 1986 (IRCA) was a subsequent U.S. immigration policy that affected the supply of labor. This policy was developed ostensibly to stem the tide of undocumented immigration to the U.S. that was stimulated by the Immigration and Reform Act of 1965 (Zolberg 1990; Griffith and Runsten 1992; Baker 1997). The IRCA legislation, in addition to introducing employer sanctions for hiring undocumented workers, made it possible for undocumented workers who could prove residency in the U.S. for a certain period of time to apply for documented status or citizenship. These developments are more commonly referred to as "amnesty" (Baker, 1997).

Within the South and Midwest regions, foreign agricultural workers had long traveled from state to state on temporary work visas. Undocumented workers also followed well-worn migration paths between states for agricultural work (Nelson 1990; Cherry 1995; Vargas 1999). Many of these workers, who had become familiar with communities in these regions from years of work in and around them settled out of farm work in response to IRCA. Many of these newly documented workers began work in downgraded manufacturing, meat- or poultry-processing, and other service sector jobs in the South and Midwest (Saenz 1991; Griffith and Runsten 1992).

Like the Hart-Celler Act, IRCA was firmly entrenched in family reunification as the basis for naturalization. Thus, the IRCA legislation kept open the pathways for family members to come to the U.S. and take advantage of the opportunity to gain documented status or citizenship (Nelson 1990; Briggs 1996). In addition to paving the way for uncounted extended family members to gain citizenship, IRCA narrowed the entryway by which those who did not have a family member who was a citizen, could enter legally.

Foreign migrant farm workers in the southeastern U.S. took advantage of the provisions of the IRCA legislation, and many began to settle out of their migrant streams and into better paying and relatively more stable industrial and manufacturing jobs. In response, a sizable increase occurred in the number of newly settled immigrants in North Carolina who had family ties outside the U.S. (Nelson 1990; Bettez 1992). The IRCA legislation made it possible for newly documented workers and new citizens to bring their family members to the U.S., as well as tell others in their communities of origin about employment opportunities and the quality of life in the American South.

Restructuring of the Economy

The economic restructuring that took off in the 1960s, accelerated in the 1980s through the fiscal retrenchment of the Reagan Era, and continues today had implications for the demand for labor worldwide. In the U.S. (and other more developed nations), restructuring was accompanied by the deconcentration of employment and population in the U.S. industrial core in the Northeast and Midwest (Bluestone and Harrison 1982; Wilson 1987). A shift occurred from unionized, high-wage manufacturing employment to low-wage high-technology manufacturing and service sector employment. In response, demographic changes within the cities also occurred. As the children of the baby boomers began to come to maturity, the number of people in the 15- to 34-year-old age cohort increased, particularly within the Black population. This dramatically increased the population of prime working-age persons and ushered in an era of labor surplus, most notably in the metropolitan areas of the U.S. Polarization of the labor force into high- and low-wage sectors was a major feature of U.S. economic development in this era (Johnson and Oliver 1989; Sugrue 1993; Wilson 1996).

Harvey reviewed these changes in terms of a shift from a Fordist mode of production to one of flexible accumulation (Harvey 1989). The shift from stable full-time employment ('cradle to grave') to part-time work, outsourcing, and subcontracting resulted in the need for a flexible, temporary workforce. He viewed these changes as part of a new configuration of the capitalist system in which bigger and more fluid markets must be found in order for business to continue procuring profit. The demand for a flexible workforce has been generated and exacerbated by this process in the U.S. This flexible workforce can easily be provided by two-way migration flows into and out of the U.S., particularly those originating in Mexico. Many immigrant workers come solely to earn money for specific periods of time with no intent to settle or naturalize.

The types of jobs made available as a result of economic restructuring have further defined employer demand. The distribution of job types drives demand for workers with certain characteristics. Employers, especially those in low-wage industries, no longer need or desire a stable, life-long workforce. An immigrant workforce can meet their more flexible needs and unskilled Hispanic immigrants are a perfect fit for many of these jobs. Therefore, economic restructuring was an unwitting precursor to an influx of unskilled immigrants. Native-born workers on the whole do not have to settle for these low-paying service jobs, especially in a healthy economy.

At the regional scale, the national restructuring of the economy manifested within the U.S. in several ways. The northern industrial belt, long the economic heart of the nation, experienced drastic declines in manufacturing employment (Bluestone and Harrison 1982; Wilson 1987; Johnson and Oliver 1989). In response to these events, major population movements accelerated within the U.S. California and points west, which had been population magnets in the past, took on a new role as population redistributors (Biggars 1979; Gober 1993). The new flexibility of production and of services allowed industries, which had been freed from the constraints of Fordist modes of production, to become more competitive and profitable, by relocating overseas. Those that could not or would not go abroad found lower overhead and better physical amenities in the suburbs of major cities in the Northeast and Midwest, and in rural areas. A major shift in locations of domestically owned and foreign-owned industries also occurred to the South region of the U.S.

Sassen's work on global cities explains recent demographic and industry changes at the local scale (Sassen 1991). In her view, restructuring of the global economy had the effect of increasingly decentralizing sites of production. Labor-intensive industries and operations were generally relocated to low wage countries and capital-intensive operations to high wage countries. Decentralization created a need for management and coordination of production to be centralized in a few key major cities. Management of global operations required high levels of technical expertise. Workers with high levels of education and technical training benefited from this phenomenon. Experts in information technology, banking, FIRE (Finance, Insurance and Real Estate), and science were very much in demand in global cities such as New York, London, and Tokyo (Sassen 1991).

The restructuring of the global economy, and especially the proliferation of foreign direct investment and financial and banking services within these global cities in the last decade, has increased the need for a flexible and low-wage workforce. The downgrading of the traditional manufacturing sector along with the casualization and informalizing of work have occurred as a part of the recent restructuring of the economy. Bifurcation of the burgeoning services sector, in terms of very high- and very low-paying jobs became the rule in many cities (Sassen 1996).

In global cities, namely New York, London, and Tokyo, native-born workers are reluctant to take low-paying jobs. This fuels demand for immigrant labor. Also within these cities, educated native-born workers monopolize occupations at the high end of the wage spectrum, therefore generating a need for many of the services that immigrant labor can provide (Sassen 1991). Jobs in the high-paying, advanced technology sector of services generate low-paying jobs (e.g. sanitation, clerking, construction, hotels, restaurants, etc.) In addition, high-income gentrification of inner city communities creates a demand for services tailored to specialized and customized needs. These services are often labor intensive.

Sassen described the same processes that Harvey called flexible accumulation (Harvey 1989). She describes a situation in which the informalization of work proliferates. Work and tasks formerly associated with the workplace are now increasingly being shifted to the household or to the community. One example of this shift is an increase in employers hiring through the social networks of current immigrant employees. This eliminates the need for extensive employer screening of prospective job applicants because the employer has found that their immigrant employees will recommend job applicants like themselves. Additionally, employers have been quoted as saying that their immigrant employees bring them higher quality workers because their own (the employee's) reputation is at stake. Moreover, experienced immigrant employees are often willing to provide on-the-job training and coaching to new recruits, thereby eliminating the need for the employer to provide these services (Waldinger 1993; Sassen 1996; Waldinger 1997).

Professionals who come to cities in response to the changing job situation create a demand for laborers who can accommodate their high-class urban lifestyles and their need for specialized and decadent services. High-income material needs (or wants) are increasingly provided by the out-sourcing of unique or short run items for eating or trendy boutiques. Low income needs can also be met by this informal approach (e.g. gypsy cab services or sweat shop production of low-priced clothing). Immigrants have historically filled these niches and continue to do so (Smith and Edmonston 1997). World systems theory also can partially explain the dramatic growth of immigrant population in non-traditional cities that have become high-tech and financial services centers e.g., Atlanta, GA, Charlotte, NC, and the Research Triangle Park, NC. The highly paid workers that have been attracted to these types of cities in recent decades have generated a need for housing and services. Immigrants, in turn, have been attracted to these areas by the abundant job opportunities.

Restructuring of the economy took on many other characteristics. Certain industries were restructured as well. The restructuring of meat- and poultry-processing, for instance, has further fueled demand for certain types of workers. These jobs are often grueling, and the reluctance of native-born workers to accept them has contributed to a shortage of willing and reliable workers in these industries. The nature of the meat- and poultry-processing industries is particularly pertinent to the situation in North Carolina (as well as to that of the Midwest) (Gouveia and Saenz 2000).

Until recently, meat-processing and meat-packing remained as it was during the time of Upton Sinclair's documentation of the Chicago packing houses in his novel, *The Jungle* (Sinclair 1906). Meat-packing houses were mainly geographically concentrated in major cities in the Midwest at the hubs of major railroads and far removed from the cattle and hog farms that supplied them. During the 1970s and 1980s, the meat-processing industry, like others, underwent massive economic and spatial restructuring. Oligopolies formed, and many companies closed their plants in the highly unionized urban Midwest. Meat-packing experienced a general geographical shift from the Cornbelt, west to the high plains (Broadway 1995). Poultry-processing had long been attracted to the southeast because of the availability of a malleable,

Theory, Immigration Policy and Demographic Change 19

low-skilled workforce, and industry-friendly local governments (Griffith and Runsten 1992; Griffith 1993) (see Figure 2-2).

Figure 2-2 Meat and Poultry Processing Plants in the US, 1998 and Percent Growth Hispanic Population, 1990-2000

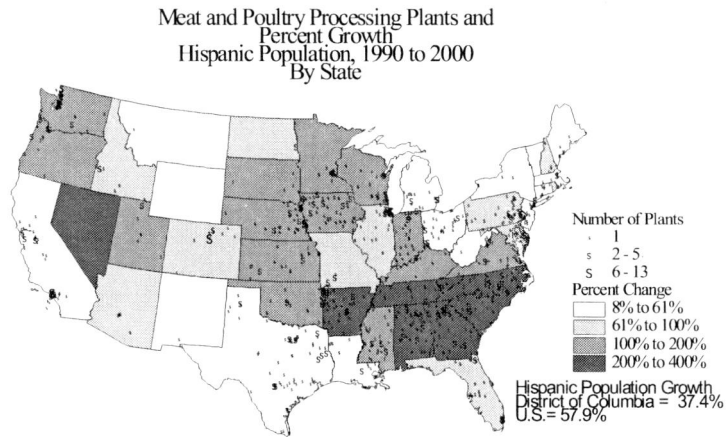

Source: U.S. Census Bureau, Census 2000 Redistricting Data (P.L. 94-171) Summary File and 1990 Census.
Produced by: Center for Policy Analysis & Public Service, Bowling Green State University.

The restructuring of the meat- and poultry-processing industries took the form of the subcontracting out of all the inputs to production. This included the outsourcing of egg hatching, the raising of livestock, and provision of grain and medicinal inputs necessary to raise livestock for processing (Hart & Mayda, 1998; Stull, Broadway & Griffith, 1995; Broadway, 1995). Arkansas, North Carolina, and Georgia together account for over 44% of poultry production in the U.S. (Broadway 1995; Carter 2002) and North Carolina is fast approaching the distinction of being the top pork producer in the nation (Grey 1995). Iowa, Minnesota, and Nebraska each have many smaller metropolitan areas and rural areas engaged in beef- and hog-processing (Gouveia and Stull 1995; Broadway 2000).

Restructuring of the meat-packing and poultry-processing industries had direct ramifications for Hispanic in-migration to North Carolina. Griffith began documenting these changes and shifts in the late 1980s and early 1990s (Griffith 1993; Griffith 1995). Employer recruiting of North Carolina Hispanics into meat- and poultry-processing was one of the precursors to dramatic demographic changes in several communities, namely Siler City in Chatham County (Levin, Rolon et al. 1995; Levin, Schlanger et al. 1995; Stocking 1998). This attracted a critical mass of Hispanics to the Piedmont Region and further fueled demand for cheap, flexible labor. Hispanics may, for a variety of reasons, have started branching out into industries other than meat- and poultry-processing as a result of being recruited to Chapel Hill, Durham, and Raleigh.

Since the meat- and poultry-processing industry was restructured in the 1970s and 1980s, immigrants, for various reasons, have made their way to non-traditional destinations in the Midwest as well, many of them as a result of these changes. Many Midwest communities have experienced significant turnarounds in their economies since the devastating deindustrialization of the 1970s and 1980s (Labich 1994; Melcher and Kelly 1994). In the early 1990s, the economies in the Midwest region of the U.S. grew at a rate faster than the national economy and their exports rose at a dramatic pace (Melcher et al, 1994). Much of this growth was due to the tremendous increase in high tech firms and "knowledge driven business" (Labich, 1994; p.88), similar to what has occurred in the Sunbelt. Chicago, one of the U.S. traditional immigrant gateways, was rated the fifth best city in the world in which to do business (Saporito 1994). Cincinnati, Cleveland, Detroit, Kansas City, Minneapolis-St. Paul, and St. Louis were all ranked relatively highly in the same *Fortune* magazine report.

Many workers, both native-born and immigrant are fleeing the poverty-ridden and crime-plagued metropolitan areas for the slower paced life in the nation's heartland. Midwestern cities such as Minneapolis-St. Paul have been reported to be ever more global in character. They contain several headquarters of transnational corporations, have a wide variety of export markets, of which its businesses are a part, and have recently experienced a dramatic change in their immigrant populations (Kaplan & Schwartz, 1996). Local and state governments in many Midwestern communities have aggressively recruited new business in order to become competitive on the global market. Additionally, although meat-processing experienced a geographical shift toward the South, this industry continues to have a major foothold in the rural Midwest. Many of these companies have recruited Hispanic workers from the traditional immigrant gateways and from abroad.

Development of the Sunbelt

In yet another regional scale development, the growth and development of what became know as the Sunbelt[3] had implications for the supply of labor and for the demand for labor in the U.S. People moving to the South in response to the movement of jobs and industry provided (and still provide) a steady stream of prospective workers. Hispanic Americans and immigrants are following suit in changing their places of settlement. They are attracted by the same amenities and plentiful jobs (albeit low-paying for the unskilled) that attract native-born workers.

A technological advance that particularly affected development in the South was the advent of air conditioning. The diffusion of air conditioning throughout the country greatly improved the attractiveness of more locations in the South for northerners. In addition, Social Security Income enabled the affluent of the retirement-age population to become "footloose." The two major U.S. retirement destinations are located in the Southeast and Southwest, in Florida and Arizona. These events, along with those discussed above, that were brought about by the restructuring of the economy, triggered the rise of the Sunbelt (Cobb 1990).

Since the Second World War, U.S. migration has been molded by the forces of post-industrialism. Population has flowed out of city centers to the suburbs and from the northeastern industrial core into the South and West regions (Berry and Dahmann 1977; Roseman 1977; Biggars 1979; Long 1988; Gober 1993; Longino 1994; Pollard and O'Hare 1999). Since the 1970s, the decade widely considered to be the watershed of change for population mobility in recent U.S. history, movement of population west and return migration to the South have been two of the major factors in the dramatic growth of the Sunbelt. Due to major job growth, especially in the South Census Region, the South has been able to retain would-be migrants, attract people who had never lived in the South, including the new "footloose" retirees, as well as return migrants (Long and Hansen 1975; McHugh 1987; Cromartie and Stack 1989; Johnson and Roseman 1990; Johnson and Grant 1997; Roseman and Lee 1998).

During the 1980s, the shift of population and industry from the Frostbelt to the Sunbelt continued with other more minor changes. The rush to the West waned, and the South was left as the premier population magnet of the country. With jobs fleeing to locations nearer the east and west coasts and from the interior of the nation to the coastal states, population redistribution in the U.S. took on a decidedly bi-coastal and coastal/interior cast (Gober 1993; Frey and Liaw 1998), which further favored the Sunbelt due to its prevalence of coastline.

The South was able to attract industry for a variety of reasons. The region had many qualities that make it ideal for labor-intensive industries, such as textile manufacturing and food processing (Biggars 1979; Cobb 1993; Bartley 1995). In addition to having a large pool of unskilled labor, the South has warm weather, relatively low energy costs, and local governments that have been historically accommodating to industry by financing industrial bonds, and providing workforce training and tax breaks, etc. The tradition of non-union labor and the enactment of "right to work" legislation were also factors that attracted industry from the North and from abroad. These were the seeds of the development of the Sunbelt.

The emergence of a global economy, regional restructuring of industry, the defense build-up of the Reagan years (which produced a "gunbelt" in the South), and a surge in improved information and communications technology each contributed to these shifts in employment and population distribution over the past 2-3 decades. Further, foreign investment became important in the Sunbelt in the early 1970s. The military spending that greatly favored the South during this period encouraged development of high technology industries and the services demanded by their employees (Gober, 1993). The general population growth in rural areas which occurred during the "Rural Renaissance" or counterurbanization of the 1970s greatly benefited the South, which is disproportionately rural (Frey 1993). This in turn created an even larger demand for goods and services and for more cheap labor in that region. Because of the phenomenal growth in high-tech jobs, those with more education and income in other regions of the U.S. turned their sights toward the South, and this in-migration greatly spurred growth in the service economy there.

The dramatic development in the Sunbelt was the catalyst for many local scale changes in the South. North Carolina is one of the states that have been transformed by the Sunbelt phenomenon. Since the mid-

1980s, North Carolina has maintained a relatively low unemployment rate. The Raleigh-Durham-Chapel Hill Metropolitan Statistical Area (MSA), which is the case study area for this study, has had an extremely low unemployment rate in recent years, even in light of the current national economic downturn. The Research Triangle Park, which is located in the Raleigh-Durham-Chapel Hill MSA, has been a magnet for highly educated workers, thus a housing boom, along with an increase in service jobs have attracted workers of all types from all over the country (Foust and Mallory 1993; Krouse 1997; Johnson 1998). Hispanics, like the rest of the U.S. population, are attracted to North Carolina by employment opportunities. In addition, North Carolina, like the rest of the Sunbelt has several amenities such as a mild climate, ocean and mountain environments, lower cost of living, and a better quality of life than is available in most of the immigrant gateway metropolises (Daniels 1997).

Recent immigration trends, including those described above that were triggered by U.S. immigration policy, have had an important regional impact on the Sunbelt South, and for the supply of labor there (Abbott 1990; Griffith 1990; Johnson-Webb and Johnson 1996; Johnson, Johnson-Webb et al. 1999). Florida, always a major destination for migrants (including retirees) and immigrants searching for work and a better quality of life, has been the cornerstone of the Sunbelt in terms of attracting large numbers of immigrants, mainly Cuban refugees (Barkan 1990; McHugh, Miyares et al. 1997). Between 1955 and 1979, immigrant populations in the Sunbelt South increased significantly, especially along what Barkan refers to as the "Miami-Honolulu axis" (1990, p. 127).

Foreign-born populations in the Sunbelt have tended to concentrate in immigrant magnet destinations or gateway communities such as Los Angeles, Houston and Miami. In 1976, California surpassed New York as an immigrant destination and has remained at the forefront as the "New Ellis Island" ever since (Waldinger 1989). Since the majority of new immigrants arrive from Latin America and the Pacific Rim, destinations that are geographically closer to these regions, like these cities, along the southern and Pacific rims of the U.S. hold a greater attraction for new immigrants and are taking predominance as ports of entry for these groups.

Immigrants are being attracted to the Sunbelt for other reasons as well. The immigrant gateway communities of "the new immigration" are disproportionately located in the South. These destinations, mainly in Florida, Texas, and California, each have long-established ethnic communities. These communities also foster migration streams by providing a supportive environment for newly arrived immigrants. Further, for immigrants arriving from Latin America and Southeast Asia, the climate in the Sunbelt is compatible with the country of origin of many of these new arrivals. Immigrants are also attracted to the economic opportunities associated with the larger Sunbelt South boom.

Employer Attitudes and Perceptions

Other factors that influence the demand for labor are employer perceptions and attitudes about the workers they want to hire. The shift to services and the dramatic increase in employment in industries such as retail, clothing manufacture, and meat- and poultry-processing (industries included in what is commonly referred to as the "competitive" sector) have increased the need for employers to use various methods to ensure or increase profitability. One of these methods is screening for certain characteristics in prospective employees. Employers' main objectives in doing this are to facilitate a harmonious workplace and increase competitiveness in establishments that interface with the public (Waldinger 1993; Waldinger 1997).

Recent research has focused on the wage gap between Black and White males, and some researchers have attributed this gap to the skills upgrading that has occurred in the past few decades as a part of economic restructuring. That is, it is believed that the wage gap is really a skills gap (Moss and Tilly 1996). Another explanation for this earnings gap is that employers have certain perceptions about Black males. Employers perceive them as not being amenable to most entry-level jobs, especially where interface with customers is frequent.

Sociologists and economists researching employer attitudes and behavior, as they affect recruitment and hiring behavior, have tended to focus on discriminatory employer attitudes and how these affect the employment prospects of Blacks, particularly Black males (Holzer 1987; Kirschenman and Neckerman 1990; Mincy 1993; Holzer 1996; Wilson 1996; Waldinger 1997; Heckman 2000). This body of research has found that due to the nature of the labor market, employers hold potential workers in a sort of mental queue based on race and ethnicity, with White workers being first in line and Black males generally at the end and Hispanic workers somewhere in the middle.

Waldinger (1993; 1997) and Holzer (1996) presented a more complicated picture, with employers generally disenchanted with native-born workers' attitudes about work and extolling the excellent work ethic of foreigners, especially Hispanics. Griffith (1995) found in his interviews of poultry plant managers that native-born workers were viewed by employers as lackadaisical with poor work attitudes. The disenchantment that employers expressed about Black males, and more generally with native-born workers, may result in a demand for the type of labor that immigrants can easily fill. Immigrants are often perceived by employers to have the right attitude toward work. They work hard and long for little pay, and as long as certain ethnic groups are kept separated, the workplace is harmonious. Additionally, immigrant workers are often used to recruit more workers with these desirable qualities, through social networks (Waldinger, 1997; 1994; 1993).

An additional aspect of employer demand for labor is the emphasis they place on "soft skills" when selecting employees. Coupled with the increasing disenchantment with native-born labor is the increasing demand by employers for "soft skills" from prospective employees as opposed to "hard skills" like education and technical training. Moss and Tilly (1996) defined "soft skills" as "...skills, abilities and traits that pertain to personality, attitude and behavior rather than to formal or technical knowledge..." (p. 253). Capelli reviewed many employer surveys and confirmed the importance employers place on such characteristics as character, discipline, personality, motivation, and attitude (Capelli 1995). Employers report that pressure to be more competitive leads to a need for employees with these characteristics (Moss and Tilly 1995; Moss and Tilly 1996). These skills are viewed as necessary for interaction in the workplace and with customers.

Although this body of research came about as a way to explain the wage gap between Black and White males, it can also lead to a better understanding of why immigrants may be in such great demand by employers. The work ethic of immigrants has been extolled in research studies and in the broader media. But this explanation also raises a contradiction, especially if immigrant workers have poor English-language skills that limit meaningful interaction with the English-speaking public. However, for "back of the house" employment, such as restaurant cooks or hotel and motel housekeepers, the preceding argument has merit.

Employers' perceptions and their demand for workers affect the modes of labor recruitment they utilize. The literature revealed the most popular methods employers use to recruit for entry-level positions. Holzer (1996) and others conducted surveys of employers and identified the most important and commonly used recruitment strategies (Capelli, 1995; Waldinger, 1997). These were: word of mouth, newspaper advertisements, and temporary agencies. Word of mouth was cited time and again as the most frequent way that a prospective employee gets a job. This has been true traditionally. However, the rise in the importance of temporary agencies is a direct response to the current demand for a flexible workforce.

North Carolina Hispanics interviewed in recent local community analyses and other related research reported that some of those who had moved there from other U.S. jurisdictions had seen a job advertisement in a local Spanish-language newspaper or had seen an advertisements on the Spanish-language television station in their area about opportunities in distant parts of the country (Bettez 1992; Griffith 1993; Levin, Rolon et al. 1995; Levin, Schlanger et al. 1995; Hedges, Hawkins et al. 1996; Cooper 1997). Previous studies have shown that employers often advertise for Hispanic workers in distant communities (Griffith, 1995; Grey, 1995; Hedges et al, 1996; Cooper, 1997). Local newspaper media sources also report that Hispanics have been recruited from out of state through these formal means.

Previous research has documented other formal and informal labor recruitment methods. Coyotes or middlemen who earn their living by escorting undocumented workers into the U.S. by various means have long been a means of entry of Mexican and other Central American workers into the U.S. labor force. These coyotes often have connections in local labor markets to help these workers get their initial job (Conover 1987). Anecdotal evidence suggests that employers often contact Mexican consulates to get information about potential workers. Temporary agencies also recruit workers for temporary assignments. Many of these agencies have begun to hire Hispanic interviewers and to advertise in the various North Carolina Spanish-language newspapers in order to tap more effectively into the supply of Hispanic workers that employers so fervently seek. Thus, employer demand for workers and their perceptions of those workers impacts how and where they recruit for workers.

Gaps in the Migration Theories

The various theories of migration discussed above each have gaps. These theories, if taken separately as explanations for the rapid influx of Hispanics to North Carolina, do not give a complete or coherent explanation for this phenomenon. The neo-classical and the "new economics" theories of migration are flawed as complete explanations of recent mass immigration to the U.S. and to North Carolina. While individual and family decisions to migrate based purely on an economic rationale or push and pull factors at the origin or destination are necessary in order for migration to take place, these factors do not completely explain the wax and wane of immigration, especially immigration from Mexico and Central America in recent history (Massey, Arango et al. 1994). The economic pull of the U.S. has always existed in stark contrast to the economic and social opportunities available in Latin America (Briggs 1984; Portes and Bach 1985), at least in the past century. Other factors have been associated with differential migration waves from Mexico, namely the Mexican Revolution (influx), the Great Depression (wane), the *Bracero* Program (influx), and the Immigration and Reform Act of 1965 (influx).

Dual labor market theory of migration addresses the direct role that the segmented market and employers play in attracting immigrant workers to this country. It is flawed because it does not explain the presence of workers' families in the U.S. If workers come solely to accrue the capital necessary to elevate their social status in their country of origin, why are so many immigrants settling in North Carolina and bringing with them their families?

World systems/global cities theory of migration is flawed in that, while urban areas of North Carolina such as, the Research Triangle Park or Charlotte, are emerging financial and cultural centers, with a burgeoning professional class and a flourishing services sector, neither can be classified as a "world city." However, economic and cultural links have been generated between the U.S. and Latin American countries, and a need for workers to fill jobs in the services sector has been generated in certain locations in North Carolina. Also, North Carolina's 2nd largest trading partner after Canada is Mexico. North Carolina has many pork- and poultry-processing plants, but, North Carolina, in particular, and the South, in general, have always had a surplus of low-wage, unskilled labor. Therefore, world systems theory does not adequately explain why immigrants would be in such high demand among North Carolina employers. But Sassen's more recent work explains immigrant concentration in low-paying jobs with terrible conditions as well as those that pay at a higher level, such as construction and furniture manufacturing (Sassen 1996). It is explained as a manifestation of the restructured global economy where a flexible, cooperative, malleable workforce is most desired by employers and firms. Immigrants, with their excellent work ethic, fill this demand perfectly, from an employer's point of view.

By considering economic, political, demographic and social factors that have contributed to the influx of Hispanics into North Carolina, this study describes the process of immigration in its temporal and spatial context. A geographical approach will view this problem in terms of relevant time periods and at different spatial scales in order to identify patterns. National, regional, and local factors have come together and continue to culminate in creating and maintaining the rapid influx of Hispanics to North Carolina in recent years. This has not been a simple process, but a rather complex one. In order to fully understand the process of migration --both international and internal-- it is necessary to view the migration process in terms of an integrative approach. If the process is to be viewed as one primarily motivated by the search for work and better pay among immigrants, then employers find themselves at the heart of the matter. Thus, this study uses Piore's (1979) theoretical framework as its foundation. Further, it appropriately analyzes other factors that have affected the demand for labor and the U.S. labor supply in recent periods.

Although Piore's (1979) dual labor market theory of migration attributes major importance to the demand for labor by employers in developed economies is a reasonable explanation for the influx of immigrants into North Carolina, it is not complete explanation. Together with neoclassical migration theory and social networks theory, a better explanation is possible, but gaps still remain. To fill the gaps in the migration theories, several other political, economic and demographic factors, which were discussed above, along with Piore's theory, give a more complete and plausible explanation for the Hispanic influx into North Carolina.

These elements have been assembled: Piore's (1979) dual labor market theory, the effects that U.S. immigration policy have had on the recent streams of immigrants to the U.S., the restructuring of the economy and the growth of the Sunbelt, and employer perceptions and attitudes as they relate to recruitment. These elements have been characterized in terms of employer demand for labor and the supply of labor, and, therefore, provide a more complete understanding of the dramatic demographic changes occurring in North Carolina. In Figure 2-1, two elements were underlined: one in the box labeled *Locational Factors* and the other in *Organizational Factors*. High-tech nodes in the South were chosen as the type of area in which to conduct the study. In this way, how these nodes have shaped and been shaped by the Hispanic influx can be explored. Further, by focusing on the recruitment behavior of employers, a deeper understanding of how the preferential hiring practices of North Carolina employers have impacted Hispanic migration to these high-tech nodes is possible.

CHAPTER 3
National Context of Hispanic Population Change

Introduction

Since well before 1848, when the U.S. government annexed a huge portion of Mexican territory through the Treaty of *Guadalupe Hidalgo* after the Mexican-American War, the Hispanic population of the U.S. has traditionally been concentrated in the Southwest. At the signing of the treaty, the people who resided in what today are the states of California, Arizona, Nevada, New Mexico, Texas and other states who were Mexican citizens, became citizens of the United States (McWilliams 1948). These traditional strongholds of Hispanic settlement, together with Illinois, Florida, New York, and New Jersey, continue to contain high proportions of the nation's Hispanic population. As Figure 3-1 shows, the majority of the U.S. Hispanic population still resides in this region.

Hispanic is an ethnic designation given by the U.S. Census Bureau (see list of definitions in Chapter 1) to persons who are from any of the Spanish-speaking Latin America countries and Spain. Hispanics of Mexican ethnicity were the largest single ethnic group in 2000 and they make up 58.5% of the Hispanic population. This is due to the proximity of Mexico to the U.S. as well as the long-standing economic relationship between the two countries. Hispanics of Mexican ancestry are still very concentrated in the southwest. The second largest group of U.S. Hispanics is the Puerto Ricans (9.6%). Puerto Ricans are considered in every way to be U.S. citizens (except that they cannot vote in the

Figure 3-1 Percent of U.S. Hispanic Population, 2000

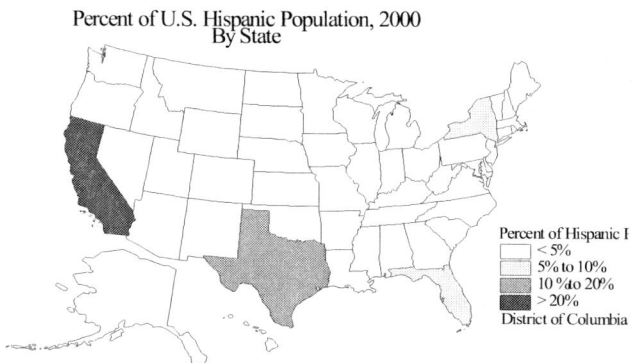

Source: U.S. Census Bureau, Census 2000 Redistricting Data (P.L. 94-171) Summary File and 1990 Census.
Produced by: Center for Policy Analysis & Public Service, Bowling Green State University.

presidential elections and are not obligated to pay income tax to the U.S. government). Puerto Ricans are concentrated in New York City and New Jersey. Cubans comprise the third largest group of Hispanics in the U.S. (3.5%). Most Cubans immigrants come to the U.S. as refugees and therefore begin their American journey on a very different footing than typical Hispanic immigrants. The U.S. Cuban population is heavily concentrated in South Florida, most notably in Miami (Boswell, Nogel et al. 2001).

The Census 2000 reveals that half of all U.S. Hispanics reside in two states: California (31.0%) and Texas (18.9%) (Guzman 2001). These two states have traditionally been and continue to be the major gateways for Hispanic immigrants to the U.S. (Gamio 1930; McWilliams 1948; Bean and Tienda 1987). The demographic and socio-economic impacts of the presence of Hispanic immigrants in these states have been widely studied and well documented in the literature (Muller 1984; Borjas 1990; Frey 1995; Johnson-Webb and Johnson 1996; Portes and Rumbaut 1996; Espenshade 1997; Johnson and Grant 1997; Smith and Edmonston 1997).

Hispanics also make up large proportions of the southwestern states (Figure 3-2). Hispanics make up 42.1% of New Mexico's population, the largest proportion in the southwest and the U.S. Arizona, which is 25.3% Hispanic, has the second largest Hispanic

Figure 3-2. Percent Hispanic Population, 2000, By State

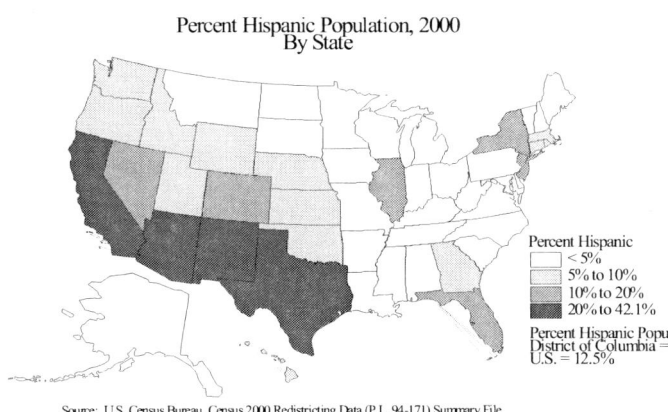

Source: U.S. Census Bureau, Census 2000 Redistricting Data (P.L. 94-171) Summary File.
Produced by: Center for Policy Analysis & Public Service, Bowling Green State University.

population, with California and Texas as a close third (32.4% and 32.0%, respectively). While the Hispanic populations of Nevada (19.7%) and Colorado (17.1%) comprise less than 20% of their respective populations, these rates are significant in relation to the rest of the states in the U.S.

Population change in the U.S. as a whole has been characterized by relatively slow growth rates. Table 3-1 shows population counts and growth rates for the U.S. and its census regions. Between 1990 and 2000 the U.S. population grew 13.2%. This rate of growth is well below that of the Hispanic population during the same period (57.9%). Regionally, the Midwest Census Region of the U.S. recorded the fastest growing Hispanic population in the nation between 1990 and 2000, 80.9% (Guzman 2001) (Table 3-1). Within this region, much of the absolute growth in Hispanic population, as in the U.S. as a whole, occurred in major metropolitan areas and the traditional immigrant gateway of the Midwest – Chicago. However, some of the largest percentage gains in Midwest Hispanic population occurred in small, rural, and ethnically homogeneous communities (these changes are notable and will be discussed in the next chapter) (Effland and Kassel 1996; Cooper 2001). The impacts of these dramatic demographic and economic changes are far-reaching for these communities as they face the challenges and opportunities these newcomers bring (Saenz 1991; Rochin 2000; von Sternberg 2001).

Table 3-1 Population Change for the U.S. and Regions,[4] 1990-2000

	Total Population 2000	Total Population 1990	Hispanic Population 2000	Hispanic Population 1990	Total % Change	Hispanic % Change	% Hispanic
U.S.	281,421,906	248,790,938	35,305,818	22,354,059	13.1%	57.9%	12.5%
Midwest	64,392,776	59,669,320	3,124,532	1,726,509	7.9%	81.0%	4.9%
Northeast	53,594,378	50,809,229	5,254,087	3,754,389	5.5%	39.9%	9.8%
South	100,236,820	85,445,930	11,586,696	6,767,021	17.3%	71.2%	11.6%
West	63,197,932	52,786,082	15,340,503	10,106,140	19.7%	51.8%	24.3%

Source: U.S. Census Bureau, Census 2000 Redistricting Data (P.L. 94-171) Summary File and 1990 Census.

Almost one quarter of the West Region's population is Hispanic, the largest proportion among the regions. This concentration exists due to the long-standing presence of Hispanics in this region and also to the fact that Los Angeles and environs are a major attraction for new immigrants, most notably Mexicans and more recently Central Americans. The region's Hispanic growth rate (51.8%), was on par with that of the U.S. Hispanic population as a whole (57.9%). The West Region also has the distinction of having the highest growth rate in total population between 1990 and 2000 (19.7%).

The Northeast Census Region was the slowest growing region of the four, both in terms of its total population (5.5%) as well as its Hispanic population (39.9%). However, the Northeast contained a relatively large share of the U.S. Hispanic population (14.8%).

The South Region had a total population of 100,236,820 and comprised 35.6% of the U.S. population in 2000. The South's population grew by 17.3% between 1990 and 2000, which is relatively higher that U.S. population growth (13.2). The South Census Region is comprised of three Census Divisions: the South Atlantic, the East South Central and the West South Central Divisions. As discussed in the previous chapter, the South has experienced an overall surge in population growth since 1980. Much of this percentage growth occurred in the East South Central and the West South Central divisions of the region.5

The Hispanic population of the South Region was numbered 11,586,696 in 2000 and this comprised 20% of the U.S. Hispanic population. The South Region also had the second highest growth rate of Hispanic population of all the Census Regions between 1990 and 2000 (71.2%). Hispanic population is distributed differentially throughout the South region and growth varied geographically as well. Table 3-2A shows total population change by census division and state for 1990 and 2000.

Table 3-2A Total Population Change in the South Census Region, 1990 and 2000

Place	1990	2000	% Change 1990-2000
South Region	85,455,806	100,236,820	17.3%
East South Central	15,176,284	17,022,810	12.2%
West South Central	26,702,793	31,444,850	17.8%
South Atlantic	43,566,853	51,769,160	18.8%
Delaware	666,168	783,600	17.6%
Maryland	4,781,468	5,296,486	10.8%
D.C.	606,900	572,059	-5.7%
Virginia	6,187,358	7,078,515	14.4%
West Virginia	1,793,477	1,808,344	0.8%
North Carolina,	6,628,637	8,049,313	21.4%
South Carolina	3,486,703	4,012,012	15.1%
Georgia	6,478,216	8,186,452	26.4%
Florida	12,937,926	15,982,378	23.5%

Source: U.S. Census Bureau, Census 2000 Summary File 1; 1990 Census of Housing and Population.

The East South Central Division is the smallest in the South Region in terms of population. Its population was 17,022,810 in 2000. Its 1990 to 2000 population growth (12.2%) was slower than the region as a whole. The East South Central Division also had the smallest Hispanic population, 299,176 (Table 3-2B). Due to the relatively small 1990 baseline Hispanic population (95,285), its Hispanic growth rate was the highest in the South (214.0%).

Table 3-2B Hispanic Population Change in the South Census Region, 1990 and 2000.

Place	1990	2000	% Change 1990-2000
South Region	6,767,021	11,586,696	71.2%
East South Central	95,285	299,176	214.0%
West South Central	4,538,985	7,043,574	55.2%
South Atlantic	2,132,751	4,243,946	99.0%
Delaware	15,820	37,277	135.6%
Maryland	125,102	227,916	82.2%
D.C.	32,710	44,953	37.4%
Virginia	160,288	329,540	105.6%
West Virginia	8,489	12,279	44.6%
North Carolina	76,726	378,963	393.9%
South Carolina	30,551	95,076	211.2%
Georgia	108,922	435,227	299.6%
Florida	1,574,143	2,682,715	70.4%

Source: U.S. Census Bureau, Census 2000 Summary File 1; 1990 Census of Housing and Population.

The West South Central had a total 2000 population of 31,444,850, making it the second largest in the region. Its total population growth (17.8%) was on par with that of the South Region (17.3%). The bulk of the Hispanic population of the South Region resides in the West South Central Division (7,043,574). This should not be surprising as Texas, the immigrant gateway of the south, is one of the states in this division. It had, however, the lowest Hispanic growth rate in the region, 55.2%.

The South Atlantic Region is the largest division in terms of population size, with a total population of 51,769,160. Its population grew by 18.8%, slightly faster than the South Region (17.3%). It had the second largest Hispanic population (4,243,946) in 2000. Its Hispanic population grew by almost 100% between 1990 and 2000. North Carolina is one of the states in the South Atlantic Division, and it contributed greatly to the high rate of Hispanic population growth in the division. West Virginia (44.6%) and the District of Columbia (which lost population overall) (37.4%) each experienced Hispanic population growth, however it was less than the national rate as well as that of the South region. Maryland and Florida each experienced Hispanic population growth below 100% (82.2% and 70.4%, respectively). The remainder of the states in this division had Hispanic population growth in excess of 100%, with North Carolina (393.9%), South Carolina (211.2%) and Georgia (299.6%) each growing more than 200%.

Table 3-3 shows the top nine southern states in terms of Hispanic population change between 1990 and 2000 compared to those states that have been traditionally consider immigrant ports of entry. North Carolina had the highest growth of all the 50 states between 1990 and 2000 (393.9%), with Georgia having the second highest Hispanic growth rate (299.6%). Moreover, of the 34 states that experienced

Table 3-3 Total Population Growth for the U.S. 1990 and 2000

Place	1990	2000	% Change
U.S.	248,709,873	281,421,906	13.2%
Immigrant Gateways	102,015,999	117,465,624	15.1%
Arizona	3,665,228	5,130,632	40.0%
California	29,760,021	33,871,648	13.8%
Florida	12,937,926	15,982,378	23.5%
Illinois	11,430.602	12,419,293	8.6%
New Jersey	7,730,188	8,414,350	8.9%
New Mexico	1,515,069	1,819,046	20.1%
New York	17,990,455	18,976,457	5.5%
Texas	16,986,510	20,851,820	22.8%
Southern Hispanic Magnets	32,671,733	41,199,966	26.1%
North Carolina	6,628,637	8,049,313	21.4
Arkansas	2,350,725	2,673,400	13.7%
Georgia	6,478,216	8,186,4523	26.4%
Tennessee	4,887,185	5,689,283	16.7%
South Carolina	3,486,703	4,012,012	15.1%
Alabama	4,040,587	4,447,100	0.1%
Kentucky	3,685,296	4,919,479	33.5%
Mississippi	2,573,216	2,844,658	10.5%
Delaware	666,168	783,600	17.6%

Source: U.S. Census Bureau, Census 2000 Summary File 1; 1990 Census of Housing and Population.

growth in Hispanic population that exceeded the national rate, 12 of these were states that are located in the South Census Region.[6] An additional 11 states that experienced relatively high percent change in Hispanic population are located in the Midwest Census Region.[7]

In comparison, several of the traditional immigrant gateways such as New York (29.5%), New Jersey (51.0%), and California (42.6%) experienced relatively lower rates of Hispanic population change compared to the nation as a whole (57.9%). It is notable that three traditional immigrant gateway states, Arizona, (88.2%), Florida (70.4%) and Illinois (69.2%), despite having rather large baseline Hispanic populations in 1990, both experienced growth in excess of the national rate. Texas, the major gateway for Mexican immigrants, also experienced a relatively high growth rate in relation to the other gateways between 1990 and 2000 (53.7%).

Redistribution of the Hispanic Population

Although a large majority of the U.S. Hispanic population resides in the Southwestern U.S., several trends in Hispanic migration began to emerge during the 1980s. Hispanics began geographically redistributing themselves to the Sunbelt South from various U.S. jurisdictions and from abroad.

Previous research, using the 1990 Public Use 5% Microdata Sample (PUMS) and census estimates foreshadowed these trends that are now being documented in the Census 2000 (Johnson-Webb, 2000; Johnson-Webb and Farrell, 1999).8 Data compiled from the 1990 PUMS file indicate that the two major domestic sources of Hispanic migration to states in the southeastern U.S. are California and Texas. New York and Florida are also well represented in the U.S. jurisdictions. Other states that served as significant redistributors of Hispanic migrants to these states include Arizona, Colorado, and New Mexico. Significant flows of Hispanics to this region also originated in Puerto Rico and abroad.

Johnson, Johnson-Webb and Farrell also found that a significant number of the Hispanics in these states have settled in metropolitan counties (1999). Atlanta, for instance, appears to be very attractive to those Hispanics arriving from Puerto Rico and from abroad.

CHAPTER 4
Midwest Context of Hispanic Population Change

Introduction
The Midwest Census Region of the U.S. recorded the fastest growing Hispanic population between 1990 and 2000 (80.9%) and is home to 8.8% of the nation's Hispanic population (Guzman 2001) (Table 4-1). Much of the absolute growth in Midwest Hispanic population, like in the U.S. as a whole, occurred in its major metropolitan areas, most notably, the traditional immigrant gateway of the Midwest, Chicago. Recently, however, streams of new Hispanic immigrants have come to rural Midwest communities. In fact, some of the largest percent gains in the Midwest Hispanic population are occurring in small, rural, and previously homogeneous communities (Effland and Kassel 1996; Cooper 2001). Many of these newcomers are finding jobs in the meat-packing and light manufacturing sectors (Johnson, Johnson-Webb et al. 1999; Nasser 2001; Sanchez 2001; von Sternberg 2001).

A Brief History
Previous research on Hispanic immigrants in the Midwest provides a rich history of those who first came in search of work on the farms and in the industrial cities of the Iron Belt at the beginning of the 20th Century (Gamio 1930; Humphrey 1943; McWilliams 1948; Cardenas 1978; Saenz and Cready 1997; Vargas 1999). After World War I, Hispanics (mostly Mexicans and Mexican-Americans) began migrating to the Midwest in response to a sharp increase in demand for labor in

the steel mills, automobile factories, the railroads, and in the rubber, electrical, manufacturing and meatpacking industries (Edson 1927; McWilliams 1948; Garcia 1979; Saenz and Cready 1997; Vargas 1999). In-migration of Hispanic workers to the region was further stimulated by the passing of the Reed-Johnson Act of 1924. This Act restricted the supply of European labor at a time when demand for unskilled labor, both in the agricultural and industrial sectors was high (Weeks and Benitez 1979). The cessation of immigration from Europe also fueled a demand for labor in the sugar beet fields of the Midwest.

The vast majority of these Hispanics who came to the Midwest came from Texas or from the Mesa Central in Mexico (Chio 1971; Carlson 1975; Haney 1979). Many of the Hispanic agricultural workers who came to the Midwest subsequently settled out of the migrant streams into industrial jobs. Railroad companies and agricultural interests extensively used recruiters to attract labor from Texas, the Southwest, and Mexico (Andrews and Nagi 1956; Vargas 1999). As a result, there exists a Hispanic-American population of significant size and duration in the Midwest.

Table 4-1 Population Change for the U.S. and Regions, 1990 and 2000.

Place	% Change Total Population 1990-2000	% Change Hispanic Population 1990-2000	% Hispanic 2000
U.S.	13.2%	57.9%	12.5%
Region			
Midwest	7.9%	80.9%	4.9%
Northeast	5.5%	39.9%	9.8%
South	17.3%	71.2%	11.6%
West	19.7%	51.8%	24.3%

Source: U.S. Census Bureau, Census 2000 Summary File 1; 1990 Census of Housing and Population.

Chicago has long been the immigrant gateway of the Midwest and indeed in it resides the largest number of Hispanics in the Midwest. However, other Midwestern communities also have a long history of Mexican and Mexican-American population. Detroit, MI; Toledo, OH;

Lorain, OH; Willmar, MN; Saginaw, Grand Rapids and Berrien Springs, MI; Milwaukee, WI; and others are but of few of the cities and towns in Michigan, Ohio and Wisconsin that have historically had relatively small but significant Hispanic populations (Macklin 1958; Carlson 1975; Faught 1976; Garcia 1979; Haney 1979; Weeks and Benitez 1979; Rosenbaum 1993; Green 1994; Fimmen, Riggins et al. 1997).

Migrant farm work continues to be a powerful attraction to the region. However many of these newcomers are finding jobs in the light manufacturing sector. The meat and poultry-processing industries, as well as other food preparation industries have been instrumental in luring immigrants to parts of the Midwest (and other regions). Since the meat- and poultry-processing industries were restructured in the 1970s and 1980s, immigrants, for various reasons, have made their way to non-traditional destinations in the Midwest (and Southeastern U.S.) (Hedges, Hawkins et al. 1996; Cravey 1997; Cohen 1998; Hart and Mayda 1998).

Hispanic immigrants who may be moving to Midwest communities because of the economic opportunities now available to them there are fulfilling a demand that has the potential to further increase economic opportunities in these communities (Humphreys 1993; Bean, Van Hook et al. 1999; Employment Policy Foundation 2001; Glick and Van Hook 2001). Immigrants may promote economic expansion by filling the demand for labor. Previous research has shown that not only do Hispanic immigrants use local public services, but they also spend money and create businesses in communities where they live (Borjas 1990; Humphreys 1993; Van Hook, Glick et al. 1999). Researchers at the Selig Center for Economic Growth projected that Hispanic buying power in the Midwest region approached $33 billion dollars in 1999 (Humphreys, 1998). In spite of the challenges faced, however, evidence exists that some communities are reaching out to their new neighbors (Howlett 1995; Ribadeneira 1996; Branson 1997; Stocking 1998; Hughes 2000) and immigrants continue to make positive contributions to their new communities (Gilbert 1996; Booth 1998; Stocking 1998; Raleigh News & Observer 1999; Rood 1999; Employment Policy Foundation 2001).

These demographic transformations have potential ramifications for the social fabric and economies of communities in the Midwest in both rural and urban communities. These implications span the provision of such public services as health care, housing and education, and more generally, for community relations and for the quality of life for both native-born residents and immigrants alike in these communities. Rural communities often lack the capacity or resources to effectively deliver services and distribute resources to their native-born residents. Experience has shown that an influx of new immigrants can put a strain on already scarce resources and this can raise tensions and conflicts in these communities Even when these population changes occur on a relatively small scale, the economic and social effects can have dramatic impacts upon these communities (Hendee 1997; Simon 1999; Glascock 2000).

Demographic Change in the Midwest

The Midwest Census Region had a total population of 64,392,776 and constituted 22.8% of the U.S. population in 2000. It is comprised of two Census divisions: the East North Central and the West North Central Divisions (Table 4-2A).

The East North Central Division has the largest population of the two regions and several of the largest metropolitan areas in the U.S. are located within it, e.g. Chicago, Detroit, Indianapolis, Cincinnati and Cleveland. The East North Central Division, with a total population of 45,155,037, has more than twice the population of the West North Central Division (19,237,739). The East North Central Division also contains 70.1% of the population of the Midwest.

Population growth in the Midwest has been modest since 1990. The Midwest grew by 7.9% between 1990 and 2000. Next to the Northeast Region (5.5%), this was the slowest growth rate of all of the census regions (Table 4-1). Of the two census divisions, the West North Central (8.9%) grew faster than the East North Central (7.5%), and exceeded the population growth rate of the Midwest as a whole (7.9%).

The 2000 Hispanic population of the Midwest numbers 3,124,532 and this is 8.8% of the U.S. Hispanic population (Table 4-B). Hispanics comprise 4.9% of the total population of the Midwest. Again, the East North Central had the largest share of the Midwest Hispanic population, 2,478,719. Almost eighty percent (79.3%) percent of the Hispanic population in the Midwest resides in the East North Central Division. Within the East North Central Division, 61.7% of the Hispanic population resides in the state of Illinois, which underscores the significance of Chicago as a port of entry to the Midwest.

Table 4-2A Midwest Total Population Change, 1990 and 2000

Place	1990	2000	% Change 1990-2000
U.S.	248,790,938	281,421,906	13.1%
Midwest Region	59,669,320	64,392,776	7.9%
East North Central Division	42,009,114	45,155,037	7.5%
Ohio	10,847,115	11,353,140	4.7%
Indiana	5,544,159	6,080,485	9.7%
Illinois	11,430,602	12,419,293	8.6%
Michigan	9,295,297	9,938,444	6.9%
Wisconsin	4,891,769	5,363,675	9.6%
West North Central Division	17,660,206	19,237,739	8.9%
Minnesota	4,375,099	4,919479	12.4%
Iowa	2,776,755	2,926,324	5.4%
Missouri	5,117,073	5,595,211	9.3%
North Dakota	638,800	642,200	0.5%
South Dakota	696,004	754,844	8.5%
Nebraska	1,578,385	1,711,263	8.4%
Kansas	2,477,574	2,688,418	8.5%

Source: U.S. Census Bureau, Census 2000 Summary File 1; 1990 Census of Housing and Population

The West North Central Division was home to 645,813 Hispanics. Hispanics, like in the Midwest as a whole, make up a relatively small proportion of the populations of both census divisions. Hispanics made up 5.5% of the population of the East North Central and 3.4% of the West North Central Division.

Midwest Hispanic population growth, like in the U.S. as a whole, exceeded total population growth between 1990 and 2000. The Midwest Hispanic population grew by 80.9%, almost ten times the rate

Table 4-2B Midwest Hispanic Population Change, 1990 and 2000

Place	1990	2000	% Change 1990-2000	% Hispanic
U.S.	22,354,059	35,305,818	57.9%	12.5%
Midwest Region	1,726,509	3,125,532	81.0%	4.9%
East North Central Division	1,437,720	2,478,719	72.4%	5.5%
Ohio	139,696	217,123	55.4%	1.9%
Indiana	98,788	214,123	116.8%	3.5%
Illinois	904,446	1,530,262	69.2%	12.3%
Michigan	201,596	323,877	60.7%	3.3%
Wisconsin	93,194	192,921	107.0%	3.6%
West North Central Division	288,789	645,813	123.6%	3.4%
Minnesota	53,884	143,382	166.1%	2.9%
Iowa	32,647	82,473	152.6%	2.8%
Missouri	61,702	118,592	92.2%	2.1%
North Dakota	4,665	7,786	66.9%	1.2%
South Dakota	5,252	10,903	107.6%	1.4%
Nebraska	36,969	94,425	155.4%	5.5%
Kansas	93,670	188,252	101.0%	7.0%

Source: U.S. Census Bureau, Census 2000 Summary File 1; 1990 Census of Housing and Population

of the total population of the Midwest (7.9%). Again, the West North Central Division had the highest growth rate of the two divisions, 123.6%. This can be attributed to a relatively small baseline population of Hispanic population in 1990. On the other hand, the East North Central Division grew by 72.4%. This growth outpaced that of the U.S. Hispanic population, however it was somewhat less than for the region as a whole.

Local Scale Demographic Change in the Midwest

Data from the 1990 Census of Population and Housing and the Census 2000 for the Midwest Region reveal several overarching trends in Hispanic population increase by county. As stated above, Hispanic population (and indeed total population) is not evenly distributed geographically throughout the Midwest, and there are sub-regional differentials as well as urban-rural differentials in both absolute and relative growth.

The largest absolute gains in Midwest Hispanic population are clustered in and around metropolitan areas of the region. Chicago and its surrounding areas, as well as Detroit, and Minneapolis metropolitan areas are at the forefront in terms of absolute increases. Several counties containing medium-sized cities such as Grand Rapids, MI; Milwaukee, Waukesha, and Madison, WI; Gary, IN; Des Moines and Sioux City, IA; Kansas City, and Wichita, KS; Kansas City and Joplin, MO; Omaha and Lincoln, NE; and Sioux Falls, SD have experienced dramatic absolute Hispanic population growth between 1990 and 2000 (U.S. Census Bureau 1990; 2000).

Percent growth in Midwest counties was also determined. These data indicate that dramatically high rates of Hispanic population growth in counties were rather widespread throughout the Midwest. The majority of counties in the region experienced Hispanic population growth in excess of the regional rate (80.9%). However, the urban and metropolitan focus of absolute Hispanic population growth turned toward rural and non-metropolitan areas of the region when considering percent change (Johnson-Webb 2001).

Within the Midwest, very definite patterns of Hispanic population growth emerged on the sub-regional scale as well. In the East North Central Division, the major metropolitan areas each experienced rates of Hispanic population growth that were on par with the national average (57.7%), but that were well below that for the region (e.g. Chicago = 54.4% and Detroit = 52.9%). Notable, however, are the extremely high rates of growth in the several of the metropolitan areas of the West North Central Division between 1990 and 2000. Minneapolis, MN (Hennepin County = 255.1%), Omaha, NE (Douglas County = 127.1%), Sioux City, IA (Woodbury County = 249.1%), and Sioux Falls, SD (Minnehaha County = 391.8%) all had extremely high rates of Hispanic population growth. Another striking feature are the dramatically high rates of Hispanic population growth in non-metropolitan or rural counties in the Midwest. These high rates are due in large part to a low baseline population of Hispanics in 1990, especially in the West North Central Division counties.

Negative Hispanic population growth in the Midwest also had a sub-regional pattern. Twenty-nine of the 39 counties that lost Hispanic population between 1990 and 2000 were located in the West North Central Division. This could be part of the general regional trend of population loss in this part of the U.S. (Rathge and Highman 1998).

Rapid demographic, social, and economic transformations such as those occurring in the Midwest region create many opportunities and challenges for rural communities that are affected by them. Research has shown that the fiscal impacts of new immigrant populations are disproportionately borne by the local communities in which they reside. When rapid demographic and cultural changes in communities are ignored or handled ineptly, this can lead to tensions and conflicts between native-born residents and newcomers. Policy makers who understand the nature of the demographic changes occurring in their communities are better equipped to make effective and relevant policy. Although the magnitude of the Hispanic presence in the Midwest may seem relatively insignificant in light of the large metropolitan immigrant gateways in other regions of the U.S., the rapid growth in Hispanic immigrant population in the Midwest has far-reaching implications for the communities involved, for the immigrants, for local government officials, service providers and for local and national policy makers.

CHAPTER 5
North Carolina Context of Hispanic Population Change

Introduction
On June 5, 1998, then-North Carolina Governor Jim Hunt signed an executive order creating the Governor's Advisory Council on Hispanic/Latino Affairs (Stawowy 1998). This act formally recognized the presence of Hispanics in the state and came as a culmination of the remarkable changes that had been occurring in North Carolina in recent years.

The media and others have documented the population explosion of Hispanics in North Carolina (Branson, 1997; Stocking, 1996; Thompson, 2002; Decierdo, 1991; Bettez, 1992 ; Glascock, 1999; Cravey, 1997; Johnson-Webb, 1996; (Johnson-Webb 1999). Since the early 1980s, Hispanics have come to North Carolina in unprecedented numbers in response to a robust economy and low rate of unemployment, many service jobs and a booming construction industry.

Background and Present Context
North Carolina is ranked 5th in terms of its percentage of Black population, and until recently, could be characterized as a state with a majority White population, with a relatively large proportion of Blacks and a small but significant population of American Indians (U.S. Bureau of Census 1993; U.S. Census Bureau 2000). After the initial settlement of Europeans in North Carolina (and indeed most of the rest

of the South) immigration was never a factor in the demographic picture. Immigrant labor was unnecessary in the South due to its legacy of the plantation economy and its long history of slavery. Even after Emancipation, North Carolina (and the South) continued to have an abundance of cheap, low-skilled labor in its newly free Black population as well as among its poor Whites, which was a hindrance to immigration in the region. The notable exception to this scenario is Florida, which has long been a gateway for Cuban and other Caribbean immigrants (McHugh, Miyares et al. 1997; Boswell, Nogel et al. 2001).

North Carolina began and continues to be a popular destination for Hispanic immigrants due to its long-term low unemployment. Figure 5-1 graphs unemployment rates for the nation, for the U.S., the South, for the South Atlantic Division and for the Raleigh-Durham-Chapel Metropolitan Area. Since 1980, North Carolina unemployment has remained very low. Even lower, the Raleigh-Durham Chapel Hill MSA (Triangle) maintained an unemployment rate of less than 2.0% for over five years. Even during the economic downturn of the last year or two, the Triangle continues to stand out (see Appendix A for a map of North Carolina counties and metropolitan areas).

North Carolina's Hispanic population traditionally has been an agrarian migrant worker population. One account indicates that Hispanics first appeared in the state as migrant workers between 20 and 25 years ago (Nelson, 1990). However, over the past twenty years, both the rate of Hispanic migration to North Carolina and the resulting settlement patterns have changed dramatically. As recently as 1990, Hispanics came to North Carolina in search of non-agricultural work.

Hispanics comprise 4.7% of the population of North Carolina according to the 2000 Census. Between 1980 and 2000, as Table 5-1 shows, the Hispanic population of North Carolina increased from 56,667 to 378,963 or by 568.8%. This rate of growth was much higher than the rates of total (36.9%), Black (30.2%), American Indian (54.0%), and non-Hispanic White population change (36.9%) in the state of North Carolina.

Only the Asian population (455.7%) in North Carolina grew more rapidly than the Hispanic population did between 1980 and 2000. However, the Asian population growth was based a much smaller absolute base than was the growth of the Hispanic population. As a consequence, the increasing Asian presence on the North Carolina landscape is much less evident than the growing presence of Hispanics.

Figure 5-1 Unemployment by Region, 1980-2000

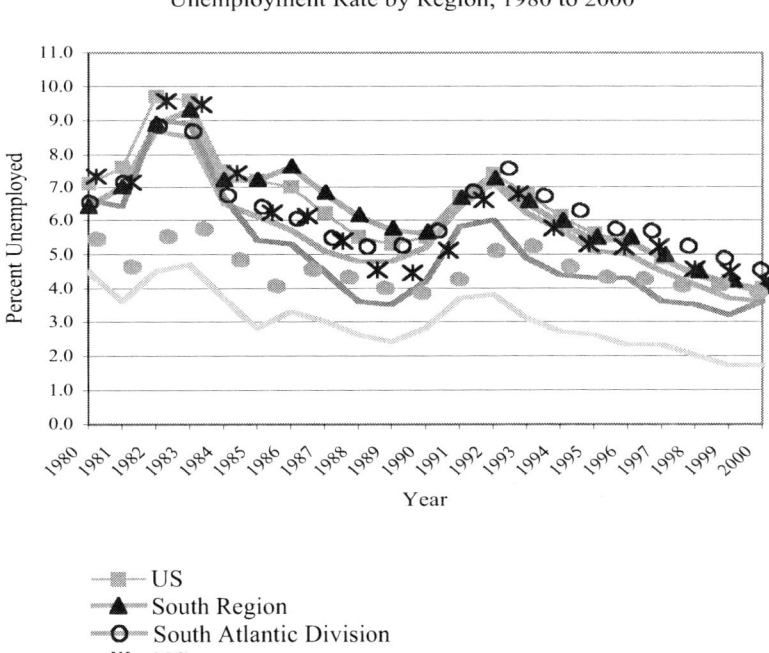

Source: Geographic Profile of Employment and Unemployment, 1983-2000; Employment and Earnings, 1980-1996; Local Area Statistics, 1981,www.bls.gov; US Department of Labor, Bureau of Labor Statistics; North Carolina Economic Trends, March, 1998, v. 4.3; 2000, v. 6.3, NC Department of Commerce. This figure has been updated from one that was first published in Johnson-Webb, 2002.

Table 5-1 Population Growth by Race and Ethnicity, 1980, 1990, 2000

Absolute Growth

	Total	White	Black	Hispanic	American Indian	Asian
1980	5,881,766	4,457,507	1,318,857	56,667	64,652	21,176
1990	6,628,637	5,011,248	1,456,323	76,726	80,155	52,116
2000	8,049,313	5,804,656	1,737,545	378,963	99,551	117,672

Percent Growth

	Total	White	Black	Hispanic	American Indian	Asian
1980-1990	12.7%	12.4%	10.4%	35.4%	24.0%	146.1%
1990-2000	21.4%	15.8%	19.3%	393.9%	24.2%	125.8%
1980-2000	36.9%	30.2%	31.7%	568.8%	54.0%	455.7%

Source: U.S. Census Bureau, Census of Housing and Population, 1980; 1990, Census 2000.

Between 1990 and 2000, Hispanic population growth in North Carolina was dramatic (393.9%). This growth is phenomenal in relation to total population growth in North Carolina (21.4%) and in comparison to the U.S. as a whole (13.2%) during the same period. The growth rate of Blacks (19.3%) in North Carolina was more in line with that of the total state population, however the White population (15/8%) grew more slowly than the total population between 1990 and 2000.

Who are the Hispanics? The Hispanic population in North Carolina, like in the U.S. as a whole is predominately of Mexican ethnicity (Table 5-2). In 2000, Mexicans and Mexican Americans comprised 65.1% of North Carolina's Hispanic population. This proportion is relatively higher than that of U.S. Hispanics (58.5). Over 8% of North Carolina Hispanics are Puerto Rican. At 9.6%, the U.S. has a slightly larger proportion of Puerto Ricans. Like in the U.S. Hispanic population, Cubans make up a small proportion of the North Carolina Hispanic population (3.5%). Other Hispanics together made up over a quarter of both U.S. and North Carolina population in 2000.

North Carolina Context of Population Change

Table 5-2 Ethnicity of Hispanics for U.S. and North Carolina, 2000

	U.S.		North Carolina	
Ethnic Group	Number	Percent	Number	Percent
Total Hispanic Population	35,305,818		378,963	
Mexican	20,640,711	58.5%	246,545	65.1%
Puerto Rican	3,406,178	9.6%	31,117	8.2%
Cuban	1,241,685	3.5%	7,389	1.9%
Other Hispanic	10,017,244	28.4%	93,912	24.8%

Source: U.S. Census Bureau, Census 2000 Summary File 1.

Figure 5-2 Age Distribution of North Carolina Population, 2000.

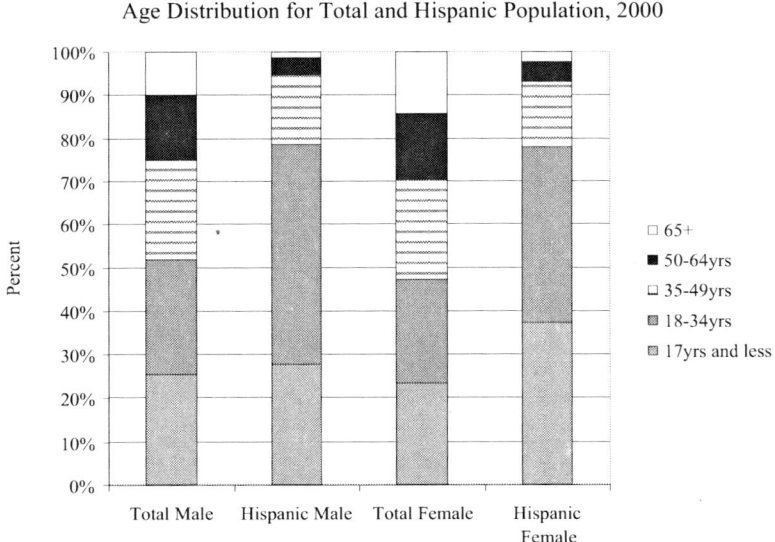

Source: U.S. Census Bureau, Census 2000.

The age distribution of the total North Carolina population and its Hispanic population is shown in Figure 5-2. This figure shows that in comparison with the total population, North Carolina Hispanics have disproportionately larger cohorts of prime working age males and females (18-34 years old). Over 50% of Hispanic males are in this age cohort. In comparison, the working age proportion comprised just 26.3% of the total state population. The North Carolina Hispanic population also has an extremely low percent of elderly population. Moreover, Hispanic females have a much larger proportion of those who are 17 years and younger (37.4%). Females out number males in the North Carolina population, with 96 males per female. However, Hispanic males outnumber Hispanic females with 148 males per 100 females. Research has shown that immigrants tend to be male, and young and the elderly tend to immigrate at rates much lower than their younger counterparts.

In order to illustrate the occupational distribution of Hispanics in North Carolina, Johnson-Webb and Johnson (1996) developed an employment profile of the Hispanic population of North Carolina using occupational data from the 1990 PUMS. While these data are a bit dated, until the 2000 PUMS are released, they are, nevertheless, the best and most reliable source of information on the statewide occupational structure of North Carolina's Hispanic population.

Hispanic occupations were grouped as defined by the Census Bureau (US Department of Commerce, 1993), into the following categories:

Primary Activities include agriculture, forestry and fisheries;

Transformative Activities include manufacturing and construction;

Distributive Services include transportation, communication, wholesale and retail trade;

Producer Services include finance, insurance, real estate (FIRE) and business services;

Personal Services include entertainment, repairs, and eating and drinking;

Social Services include medical, education and government;

Active Military includes active status in a branch of the US military.

Contrary to preconceived notions of Hispanic agricultural employment North Carolina Hispanic workers were widely dispersed throughout the North Carolina economy in 1990. Compared to the statewide distribution of workers, North Carolina Hispanics were as over-represented in what are typically considered to be low-wage occupations--primary activities and personal services--as they are in other communities outside in North Carolina which have a substantial Hispanic presence. But unlike in many other such communities, they were also over-represented in social services and the military, occupations that pay better wages. In addition, although they were under-represented by statewide standards, there was substantial representation or presence of Hispanics in transformative activities, especially construction, where the wages are fairly high.

Where have Hispanics settled in North Carolina? Between 1980 and 2000, most Hispanics settled in the state's metropolitan communities along the I-85 corridor and in those encompassing the state's military bases (Figure 5-3). However, since 1990, nonmetropolitan counties have accounted for some of the most rapid Hispanic population growth rates,
suggesting that Hispanics are settling throughout the state--in rural and urban communities alike (Figure 5-4).

Where did the Hispanic newcomers to these metropolitan areas originate? The data needed to answer this question, especially for those Hispanics arriving since 1990, must await the publication of the 2000 PUMS data. However, a partial answer can be gained from data contained in the 1990 Public Use Microdata 5% Sample file, as well as that from the 2000 Supplemental Survey of the Census Bureau. These data indicate that Hispanic newcomers to North Carolina originated in other U.S. jurisdictions and from abroad. In Figure 5-5, the 1990 PUMS was used to show, that the largest flows originated in traditional Hispanic gateways such as New York, Illinois, California and Texas. During this period there were also salient flows to the state from Puerto Rico and abroad.

The 2000 Supplemental Survey data, however, provide a hint of the states from which North Carolina Hispanics have come more recently.9 Table 5-3 illustrates the origins of North Carolina Hispanics who had just arrived in the state. The results indicate that Hispanics, between 1999 and 2000 came from many of the same jurisdictions as did those who came to the state between 1985 and 1990. Arizona sent the largest number of Hispanics to North Carolina (9,335) between 1999 and 2000. Interestingly, the next two states that sent the most

Hispanics to North Carolina are located in the Southeast: Georgia (6,899) and Florida (6,744). California also sent a significant

Figure 5-3 Distribution of North Carolina Hispanic Population, 1990 and 2000

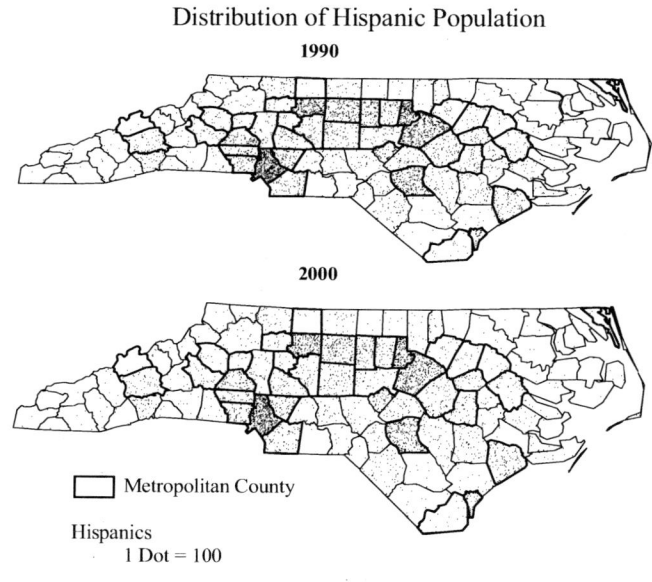

Note: Dots are placed randomly within states.
Source: U.S. Census Bureau, Census 2000 Summary File 1; 1990 Census of Population and Housing.
Produced by: Center for Policy Analysis & Public Service, Bowling Green State University.

number of Hispanics (6,622) to North Carolina and New York sent an additional 1,164 Hispanics.

As far as international origins, Mexico stands out overwhelmingly, with 14,192 Hispanics reporting that they lived there in 1999. However, over 7,000 Hispanics immigrated to North Carolina from other countries in Latin American (2,604) and South America (4,466) as well. What is interesting about these results is that the state of Texas, the largest port of entry for Mexican immigrants is notably absent from the list of states from which Hispanics reported they came. This aspect of the results is dramatically different from those obtained in the 1990 PUMS, in which Texas was a major point of origin for North Carolina Hispanics who moved to the state between 1985 and 1990. This disparity is no doubt due to the very small sample of Hispanics that were surveyed; none of those captured in it indicated Texas as a point of origin in 1999.[10]

Figure 5-4 Percent Growth in North Carolina Hispanic Population, 1990-2000

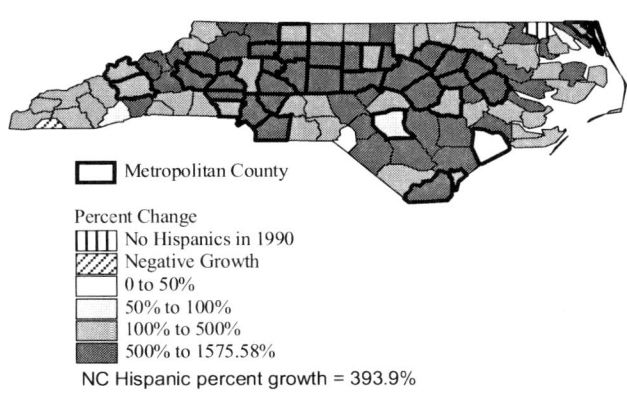

NC Hispanic percent growth = 393.9%

Source: U.S. Census Bureau, Census 2000 Summary File 1;
1990 Census of Population and Housing.
Produced by: Center for Policy Analysis &
Public Service, Bowling Green State University.

Table 5-3 Origin of Hispanic In-Migrants to North Carolina, 1999-2000

Place	Number of Hispanic In-Migrants
From Abroad	21,262
Mexico	14,192
Latin America	2,604
South America	4,446
U.S. Jurisdictions	
Arizona	9,335
Georgia	6.899
Florida	6,744
California	6,622
New York	1,164
Total	52,026

Note: Another 88,367 Hispanics are estimated to have lived in another NC county in 1999.
Source: U.S. Census Bureau, 2000 Supplemental Survey, CS202 Data.

Other Indicators of the Growing Presence of Hispanics in North Carolina

Everywhere the effects of the rapid influx of Hispanics on North Carolina communities have become apparent. City bus schedules have been translated into Spanish and automatic teller machines now have a Spanish-language option. The local Chapel Hill, NC newspaper now publishes a regular section of the paper in Spanish (Assiss 2002). The North Carolina Department of Motor Vehicles (DMV) publishes its driver education manual in Spanish and encourages all of its examiners to learn Spanish in order to better serve the growing Hispanic population (Sheehan 1999). *El Pueblo*, Inc., a relatively long-standing Hispanic advocacy group based in Chapel Hill, has held a Hispanic voter registration drives. Community health centers and hospitals display signage that has been translated into Spanish. Community colleges throughout the state have added English as a Second Language

Figure 5-5 In-Migration Fields of Hispanics to the Triangle, 1985-1990.

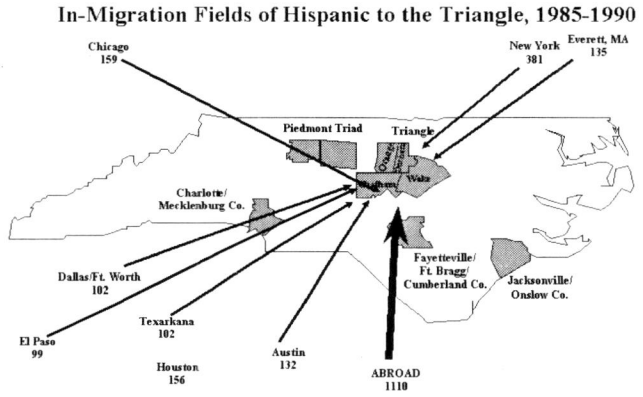

classes, most of which are filled to capacity. Many of these institutions also offer assistance to employers by providing classes for supervisors in basic Spanish and cultural sensitivity. Several more indicators of the growing presence of Hispanics in North Carolina exist and are described below.

The most recent county-level birth statistics provide an indicator of the great potential for Hispanic population growth in North Carolina. In 1999, as Figure 5-6 illustrates, the highest percentages of births to Hispanic parents were concentrated in four of the state's non-metropolitan counties: Duplin (31.4%), Lee (31.8%), Montgomery (24.2%), Sampson (24.0%). In each of these counties, the Hispanic proportion of all births was significantly higher than the Hispanic proportion of all births in the state in 1999 (8.7%). In only one of the state's metropolitan counties--Chatham (20.8%), was the proportion of Hispanic births significantly higher than the statewide proportion.[11] Given that most of the adult Hispanic newcomers are in their childbearing years, the foregoing statistics suggest that the Hispanic population will continue to grow and disperse throughout the state in the years to come (Johnson, Johnson-Webb et al. 1999).

Figure 5-6 Percent of Births that were Hispanic, 1999, By County

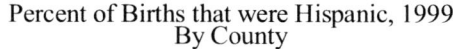

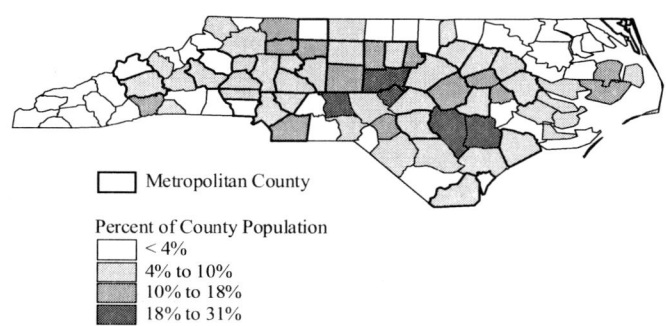

Percent of County Population
- < 4%
- 4% to 10%
- 10% to 18%
- 18% to 31%

Source: www.ayudate.org/ayudate/County Demographics.html; accessed 12/9/00, 023:00:46p.m.
North Carolina Center for Health Statistics, NC Selected Vital Statistics, v.1, 1999;
www.schs.state.nc.us/schs/healthstats/vitalstats/volume1-99; accessed 12/10/01, 12:51:34p.m.
Produced by: Center for Policy Analysis & Public Service, Bowling Green State University.

The distribution of meat- and poultry-processing plants in North Carolina are yet another indicator of the growing presence of Hispanics in the state. Research has shown that workers in many of these plants are now a majority Hispanic workforce (Levin et al, 1995a; 1995b; Griffith, 1990). A visual correlation between the locations of meat- and poultry-processing plants and percent change in Hispanic population by county is provided in Figure 5-7. These plants are concentrated in the Piedmont and Coastal Plain regions of the state, in metropolitan (mainly in the Piedmont) and nonmetropolitan (mainly in the Coastal Plain) areas.

The growing presence of Hispanic owned businesses on the North Carolina landscape is yet another indicator that the state is undergoing a drastic change in its racial and ethnic makeup. A recent report, estimated that North Carolina Hispanics have the purchasing power of $2.3 billion dollars (Humphreys 1993). This is not an insignificant contribution to the economy of the state and most of these businesses have been formed to serve the emerging market needs of the Hispanic newcomers.

Figure 5-7 Hispanic Population Growth, 1990, 2000 and Locations of Meat and Poultry Processing Plants, 1998, in North Carolina Counties

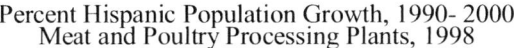

Percent Hispanic Population Growth, 1990- 2000
Meat and Poultry Processing Plants, 1998

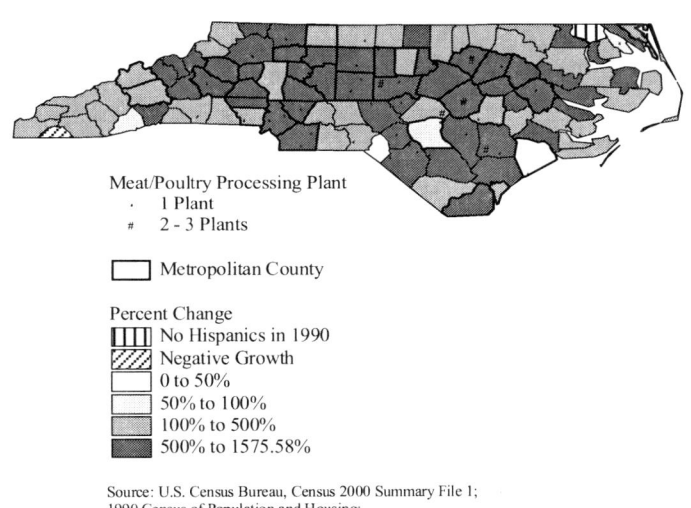

Meat/Poultry Processing Plant
. 1 Plant
2 - 3 Plants

☐ Metropolitan County

Percent Change
▦ No Hispanics in 1990
▨ Negative Growth
☐ 0 to 50%
▤ 50% to 100%
▥ 100% to 500%
■ 500% to 1575.58%

Source: U.S. Census Bureau, Census 2000 Summary File 1;
1990 Census of Population and Housing;
World Pages,Web YP Inc., 1998, www.worldpages.com/bus/
Produced by: Center for Policy Analysis
& Public Service, Bowling Green State University.

In 2000, unofficial estimates placed the number of Hispanic-owned businesses in the state at 700. The Triangle reportedly has some 150 of these businesses (Raleigh News & Observer 1999).

To date, twenty-one Spanish-language newspapers or magazines are published within the state. Five of these are targeted toward the Triangle area market. Two are based in Raleigh. Among the Raleigh papers, *La Conexión* is targeted to the working class Hispanic population and the other, *La Voz de Carolina* is geared more toward the educated middle class. *Popular*, published in Charlotte is a Spanish-language-magazine (Robles 1997; Ayudate 2002). In addition to

Spanish-language print media, there are 33 radio shows that are produced for North Carolina Hispanics.

Efforts to start a Latino credit union began in Durham, NC in 1997 (Bickley 1999). The Latino Credit Union opened its doors in June of 2000. A Hispanic chamber of commerce has also been established to serve Hispanic-owned and other businesses seeking to tap into the burgeoning Hispanic market.

In addition to businesses and business support organizations, a number of other Hispanic organizations have formed to address the social and economic needs of the state's growing Hispanic population. One such organization is the North Carolina Society for Hispanic Professionals. Its mission is to improve educational opportunities and outcomes for Hispanic youth. In 1998, then-North Carolina Governor Jim Hunt created the Hispanic/Latino Task Force as part of his Office of Minority Affairs. However, prior to the formation of the Task Force, several Hispanic community service and advocacy groups had already formed. The web page of the Hispanic/Latino Task Force formerly listed 43 Hispanic organizations within the state (State of North Carolina, 2000). At least thirteen of these organizations operated in the Triangle area.

As of 2002, however, *Ayudate* reports that there are now 124 organizations in the state that serve the Hispanic population. This represents a threefold increase in two years. Forty-six of these organizations operate in the Triangle area (Ayudate 2002).

Hispanic soccer leagues have grown very rapidly in North Carolina. The North Carolina Amateur Soccer Association (NCASA) has among its membership no less than five Hispanic leagues. *La Liga de Raleigh* is located in Raleigh, NC (NCASA 2002). The North Carolina Hispanic leagues play an annual tournament championship in Raleigh. In 2000, the Raleigh Police Department, in order to facilitate relations with the Hispanic community, began holding the *Festival de las Americas* (Schulman 2000). This festival hosted a soccer tournament, and provided ethnic foods and entertainment. The Capitol Area Soccer League, a mainstream league, hired a publicity director to forge a relationship with the local Hispanic community in hopes of recruiting good soccer players. Several local high schools have also reported that their varsity soccer teams have been much improved by the addition of Hispanic immigrant student athletes (Carter 1999).

The growth in Hispanic soccer teams and leagues have stretched the local Parks and Recreation Department resources to the limit

(Schulman, 2000). As a result of community tensions in Orange County, NC (which contains the town of Chapel Hill) involving use of public facilities by diverse groups, the Orange County Board of County Commissioners appointed a task force to organize and host the Orange County Soccer Symposium in April 2000 (Board of Commissioners, 2000). The purpose of this symposium as stated by the news release was to explore "...what facilities are currently available, what is needed, what are the possibilities of diverse soccer leagues working together, what sorts of arrangements are required to share usage of fields, and what private and public funding sources are available" (County Commissioners 2000). Speakers included the soccer coach from University of North Carolina at Chapel Hill, a County Commissioner, a Carrboro, NC Alderman, a Chapel Hill Town Councilman and a Hillsborough, NC Town Commissioner. Representatives of the various soccer leagues operating in Orange County and a representative of informal Hispanic soccer teams also participated in a panel discussion about the demand for soccer in the county.

The growing presence of Hispanics in North Carolina has prompted several major changes in the state's institutional framework. North Carolina has had a Hispanic Ombudsman for several years and an Honorary Consul of Mexico has resided in Charlotte for close to twenty years. North Carolina is under the 6-state jurisdiction of the General Consulate of Mexico in Washington, D.C. In response to the staggering growth in Hispanic population in the state, and as a result of the demand for services generated by the growing Mexican population, the Consulate began to conduct mobile consulates in various locations throughout North Carolina with increasing frequency in the late 1990s. In 2000, the Consul General of Mexico in Washington, D.C., Ministro Juan Carlos Cué Vega, announced that the government of Mexico planned to establish the first full Mexican consulate in North Carolina in Raleigh. Ministro Cué also reported that this full consulate would relieve the honorary consulate in Charlotte of the overwhelming load it had been carrying (Eisley 2000). The Mexican Consulate in Raleigh was opened in November of 2000.

In 2000, the Immigration and Naturalization Service (INS) set up a "rapid response team" in Raleigh. The Charlotte office, formerly the sole office in North Carolina, housed four agents who were responsible for several states. At that time the Charlotte office was upgraded to include ten agents. The INS subsequently opened a new office in Winston-Salem, which has three agents. The new office in Raleigh has five agents and its jurisdiction is the eastern portion of the state. The opening of this office coincided with a push by the U.S. Census Bureau and many North Carolina Hispanic advocacy groups to encourage Hispanics, regardless of their documentation status, to be counted in the 2000 census. The timing was perceived by some community advocates to have been poor, resulting in the heightening of fears of undocumented Hispanic workers. Many thought that this would result in this segment of the community avoiding the census and thus, being significantly undercounted (Glascock 1999).

In 1999, then-Governor Hunt appointed the first Hispanic person in North Carolina history to the state board of education (Wagner 1999). This appointment was a clear indication of the dramatic rise of Hispanic student enrollments in North Carolina public schools. Data collected by the North Carolina Department of Public Instruction revealed that approximately 33,000 Hispanic children enrolled in North Carolina public schools in the 1997-98 school year. This constituted a rate of change in enrollments of 250% over a one-year period. Some local school districts reported at that time that up to 40% of grades K-3 were Spanish-speaking students. In the 1999-2000 school year, the number of Hispanic children enrolled in North Carolina school reached 46,168 a 40% increase since 1997-1998 (NCCHS 1999).

In many school districts where this rapid growth in enrollments has occurred, these new arrivals have stretched resources for English as a Second Language classes in public school to the breaking point. In Siler City, NC (located in Chatham County), for example, many long-term residents reportedly moved their children to other district schools in response to the rapid influx of Spanish-speaking students into their school districts. Some of these community members feared for the quality of their children's education as their teachers struggled to accommodate the language barrier (Reddy 1999).

Community Attitudes

These changes have not come without a price. Considerable tensions and conflicts over jobs, housing, schools and other goods and services have often accompanied the influx of Hispanic newcomers into traditional immigrant gateways (Oliver and Johnson 1984; Johnson and Oliver 1989; Johnson, Farrell et al. 1997). In the 1990s, evidence existed that these same types of tensions and conflicts had emerged in North Carolina. Since the events of September 11, 2001 and the subsequent economic downturn, tensions in North Carolina communities, like those in others across the nation have increased in response to the demographic changes that are occurring (Reddy 1999; Glascock 2000; DeJong and Tran 2001; Hull 2001; Thompson 2001; Hull 2002; Ross, Hart et al. 2002).

In an effort to systematically gauge public attitudes toward Hispanic newcomers, Johnson-Webb and Johnson (1996) analyzed data from the 1996 Spring Carolina Poll (IRSS, 1996). The poll posed, among others, the following four questions to a representative sample of 655 North Carolinians:

How comfortable are you with the influx of Hispanics into the state?

How would your neighbors feel about Hispanics moving into your neighborhood?

How comfortable are you around people who are not speaking English?

How comfortable are you with the influx of Northerners into the state?

Results of this analysis are summarized here. Table 5-4 provides detailed results of the 1996 analysis. In general, North Carolinians harbored negative feelings about the influx of Hispanics into the state. Nearly half of respondents said they were uncomfortable with the increasing presence of Hispanics, 67% said they thought their neighbors would not approve of Hispanics moving into their neighborhood, and over half (55%) said they did not feel comfortable around people who do not speak English. Such sentiments were not expressed at such high levels, however, against Northerners. Only 26% of the respondents said the influx of Northerners made them uncomfortable.

North Carolinians who had no high school diploma, those who were unemployed and those who lived in metropolitan areas were significantly more negative about the Hispanic influx. Long-term residents harbored significantly more negative attitudes about

Table 5-4 Results of Carolina Poll, Spring, 1996

		Negative Attitude Toward Latino Influx	Neighbor Would Be Negative about Latino Influx
All Respondents		48%	41%
High School	Yes	35%	64%
Graduate	No	49%*	71%
Employment Status	Full-time	44%*	70%
	Part-time	29%	71%
	Unemployed	60%	60%
	Other	39%	63%
Race	Black	38%	54%*
	White	44%	69%
	Other	26%	55%
Gender	Male	44%	70%
	Female	40%*	65%
Metropolitan Residence		39%*	66%
Nonmetropolitan Residence		45%	69%
Coastal Plain Resident		35%*	65%*
Piedmont Plain Resident		45%	66%
Mountain Resident		37%	67%
Lived in NC at age 16?	Yes	49%*	70%
	No	26%	59%
Is Respondent a Southerner?	Yes	46%*	68%
	No	28%	62%

Source: Carolina Poll, Spring, 1996; School of Journalism and Institute for Research in the Social Sciences, University of North Carolina at Chapel Hill. * Statistically significant.

Table 5-4(cont.) Results of Carolina Poll, Spring, 1996

		Negative about Non-English-Speaking	Negative about Influx of Northerners
All Respondents		55%	26%
High School	Yes	50%	22%
Graduate	No	59%*	28%
Employment	Full-time	41%*	27%*
Status	Part-time	50%	35%
	Unemployed	33%	13%
	Other	42%	16%
Political	Democrat	46%	50%
Affiliation	Republican	66%	32%
	Independent and Other	53%*	40%
Registered to vote	Yes	56%*	27%
	No	52%	24%
Lived in NC at	Yes	58%	30%*
age 16?	No	47%	13%
Is Respondent a	Yes	58%	28%
Southerner?	No	46%	17%

Source: Carolina Poll, Spring, 1996; School of Journalism and Institute for Research in the Social Sciences, University of North Carolina at Chapel Hill. * Statistically significant.

Hispanics and Northerners. However, the levels of opposition to the influx of Northerners were not as high as the levels of concern about the influx of Hispanics.

Neighborhoods that were formerly predominately Black have become increasingly inhabited by Hispanics in a matter of months. Many of the Blacks who inhabited these communities felt uncomfortable with the growing presence of Hispanics. As a result, community groups representing both groups came together to try to address these tensions (Stocking, 1997b). Tensions and conflicts have arisen, especially where the residential areas of Blacks and Hispanics meet and these have been reported in the local media (Stocking 1997; Stocking 1997).

El Centro Hispano got the Hispanic community involved with the Durham police department after several hate crimes were perpetrated against members of that community. Hispanics in Durham became victims of home invasion robberies by Black assailants that also included beatings and sexual assaults. It was reported that some criminals view Hispanic immigrants as easy targets due to the perception that they horde large amounts of cash either on their person or in their homes (Kane 1988; Garrett 1997).

Recently, in Siler City, David Duke, former Grand Wizard of the Knights of the Ku Klux Klan, held a demonstration under the rubric of a new organization he has formed called the National Organization for European American Rights (NOFEAR) (Glascock 2000). There was a small turn out of protesters who were angry about the "invasion" of their community by undocumented workers. Many more hundreds of people showed up in counter protest.

Close to one half of North Carolina Hispanics live within the urban communities along the I-85 corridor (Johnson-Webb and Johnson 1996). The I-85 corridor lies predominately within the Piedmont Region of North Carolina. Residents of this region expressed significantly negative attitudes toward the influx. Nonmetropolitan respondents had more negative attitudes toward Hispanics than did metropolitan respondents. This may be fortunate for a large proportion of Hispanics, who are concentrating in metropolitan areas within North Carolina. However, the dramatic growth in nonmetropolitan areas that can be expected due to natural increase is likely to spark ethnic tensions in those communities. The fact that unemployed and uneducated North Carolinians were so negative about the Hispanic influx suggests that ethnic tensions surrounding the labor market are festering in North Carolina, and could be exacerbated by the current economic downturn.

Aside from the negative attitudes expressed by some North Carolinians, positive reactions also have also taken root. Community service organizations geared toward Hispanics have flourished. Both traditional and Hispanic community organizations and human relations commissions have come together to deal with specific issues relating to the influx. The size of the counter-protest in Siler City attests to the presence of community members who are supportive of the Hispanic community. One of the most important positive aspects of the influx is that Hispanics are filling the huge demand for unskilled labor. Additionally, they are generating wealth and creating new businesses within the state (Krouse 1997; Stevens 1999; Hughes 2000; Nasser 2001).

CHAPTER 6
Research Methods

The Study Area

The Research Triangle region of North Carolina (for the purposes of this study, Orange, Durham, Chatham and Wake Counties; see Appendix A) was selected as the case study context for this research because it has taken on the characteristics of a "world class" community over the past quarter century, as postulated by global cities/world systems theory (Sassen, 1991).

Beginning in the 1970s and 1980s, and accelerating throughout the 1990s, the Research Triangle Park, and the I-85 corridor more generally, emerged as a major magnet for employment growth (Eisenstadt, 1997; Foust and Mallory, 1993), especially in high technology manufacturing and related business services. This growth was fueled by the state's pro-business climate, its mild weather, and its many other amenities, which, in turn, led to a major influx of highly-educated professionals, a boom in residential and commercial construction, and a sharp increase in the demand for both business and personal services (Krouse, 1997; Cobb, 1993). In part as a function of these developments, by 1975, the Raleigh-Durham-Chapel Hill MSA was heralded as having more Ph.D.s per 100,000 population than any other U.S. city of its size (Foust and Mallory, 1993). Owing to an increasingly tight labor market, the Triangle began to be recognized as a newly emerging magnet for Hispanic in-migration and settlement by the mid-1980s. By the mid-1990s, the Triangle had achieved the status of the one of the strongest magnets for Hispanic population growth in the state (MDC 2002). Moreover, in their study of immigration growth in U.S. metropolitan areas, Suro and Singer designated the Raleigh-Durham-Chapel Hill MSA as one of the country's "hypergrowth new Latino locations" in terms of its dramatic increase in immigrant population (Suro and Singer 2002).

Geographic proximity was another factor in the selection of the Research Triangle as the case study context for this study. Its proximity to the University of North Carolina at Chapel Hill, where the research was analyzed, made data collection more practical and affordable.

Data Collection Strategy and Methods

The goal of this part of the study was to determine the extent to which Triangle employers used: (a) media advertising (newspaper, radio, and television) locally and in major immigrant gateway communities and (b) local, regional, national, and international employment intermediaries to lure Hispanic labor to the Triangle. Toward these ends, a content analysis of major newspapers in immigrant gateway cities was undertaken, and key informant interviews were conducted with selected media personnel in gateway cities, and locally with employment intermediaries and a group of employers.

Newspaper Content Analysis

Johnson-Webb and Johnson (1996), using the 1990 Public Use Microdata 5% Samples (PUMS) identified specific Hispanic in-migration fields to North Carolina. Figure 5-5 illustrated the in-migration fields into the Triangle between 1985 and 1990.[12] The following cities were identified as the major U.S. cities from which Hispanics came to North Carolina: El Paso, Dallas and Houston, TX; Chicago, IL; New York, NY; and Boston, MA (Everett).

In order to determine whether North Carolina employers had advertised for Hispanic workers in newspapers in these communities, efforts to secure the major Spanish-language newspaper in each of these cities were undertaken. This investigation revealed that Spanish-language newspapers in these sending communities were not available through interlibrary loan and therefore could not be used in this study. In view of this situation, a decision was made to analyze the out-of-state job advertisements in the major English-language newspapers in these communities.

The newspapers that were sampled in this study were identified using *The Gale Directory of Publications and Broadcast Media*

(Fischer, 1998). These publications included: the *New York Times*, the *El Paso Times*, the *Dallas Morning News*, the *Houston Chronicle*, the *Boston Globe*, and the *Chicago Tribune*. Microfilm issues of the *El Paso Times*, the *Dallas Morning News*, and the *Houston Chronicle* were obtained through interlibrary loan. The *New York Times*, the *Boston Globe*, and the *Chicago Tribune* were available in the microfilm section of the Walter Royal Davis Library at the University of North Carolina at Chapel Hill.

One goal of this phase of the research was to determine if there were identifiable trends in out-of-state advertising by North Carolina employers. Toward this end, three specific years were selected as the sampling time frames for the newspaper content analysis: 1980, 1988, and 1996. The early 1980s were a period of rapid economic and employment growth in the South, which created the climate for large-scale migration to communities like the Research Triangle. The midpoint of the study period, 1988, was selected in order to measure any change in advertising over time. Also, the Immigration Reform and Control Act of 1986 (IRCA) may have had an impact on formal recruitment for Hispanic labor to North Carolina. Immigrants that were able to take advantage of the IRCA provisions were either documented by this time or well on their way to being documented. The change in documentation status for this population might have influenced their choice of job and migration behavior as well as their desirability among employers. The end point of the study period, 1996, was chosen because Hispanic migration to North Carolina cities was in full motion by this time. For these three time periods, two months were selected at random (June and November), and for both months, the Sunday papers (in each case, the largest circulation day) were selected for the purpose of conducting the content analysis of out-of-state employment advertising for Hispanic labor.

Because Waldinger (1997; 1993) and others have documented that immigrants often are concentrated in low-wage, services employment, newspaper advertisements classified under Trades or Skilled Trades, General, Miscellaneous, Restaurants, Lounges, Hotels and Clubs, and Domestic were reviewed for this study. Advertisements in the Professional, Health, Sales, Clerical, Professional Degree Required, etc., sections were not included in this analysis. When a relevant advertisement was found, it was typed verbatim into an Excel® spreadsheet along with the name and date of the newspaper and the classification of the ad. Several of the advertisements were photo copied as well. Subsequently, the advertisements collected were reclassified using the occupational typology described in Chapter 5 which revealed that most of them fell under one of three categories: primary activities, transformative activities or personal services. Once the reclassification was completed, the results of the newspaper content analysis were tabulated for further analysis and interpretation.

Key Informant Interviews

To ascertain additional information on employer recruitment strategies, interviews were conducted with Spanish-language newspaper, radio, and television advertising personnel in the gateway cities that were selected above. Consular officials were also interviewed in several of these cities. Locally, interviews were conducted with North Carolina Employment Security Commission (ESC) and temporary agency personnel, and a group of North Carolina-based employers. The strategies used to identify the key informants in each of these categories are described below.

Hispanic Media Personnel

Because Spanish-language newspapers were not available via interlibrary loan, telephone interviews with key informants in the newspaper, radio, and television industry were deemed an acceptable alternative to get information about employer recruitment practices in those media. The most popular Spanish-language media in the communities identified as major redistributors of Hispanic population to North Carolina's Research Triangle (i.e., El Paso, Dallas and Houston, TX, Chicago, IL, New York, NY, and Boston, MA [Everett]), were selected from a search of the World Wide Web, *The Gale Directory of Publications and Broadcast Media* (Fischer 1998), the *Hispanic Resource Directory* (Schorr 1992), and the *Hispanic Americans Information Directory* (Furtaw 1992). Subscriptions were also purchased for the major Spanish-language newspaper in each of these cities. These sources were consulted to identify (a) the most prominent Spanish-language television, radio, and newspaper outlets in each city and (b) the names and contact information for advertising personnel in these companies.

Once possible key informants were identified, each of them were sent a letter of introduction, two sample research publications on the growing Hispanic population of North Carolina, a consent form, and a self-addressed stamped envelope. Typically, after a week or so, a telephone call was placed to see if the potential respondent was interested in being a part of this research. If the respondent agreed to participate in the study, he or she was either interviewed on the spot, or a time was set up to call back that was mutually convenient.

Table 6-1 Description of Those Interviewed for this Study*

Source of Interview	# of Interviews Solicited	# Interviews Completed	Average Number of Years Experience	Range of Years of Experience
Spanish Television Personnel	6	4	14.3	5-31
Spanish Radio Personnel	5	2	12.5	12-33
Spanish Newspaper Personnel	5	4	19.0	3-33
Mexican Consular Officials	7	5	9.0	1.75-18
Employment Security Commission	4	4	24.6	23.5-26
Employers	12	7	7.9	1-23
Total	39	26	16.6	1-33

*This table was first published in and adapted from Johnson-Webb, 2002, p. 413.

A total of ten interviews were completed with personnel from Spanish-language newspapers, television and radio stations in New York, El Paso, Dallas, Houston, Chicago and Boston (Table 6-1). Of six interviews solicited at television stations, four were completed. Of five radio stations solicited, two interviews were completed. Of the five newspapers contacted, four interviews were completed.

As far as geographic coverage, interviews were completed with at least one media source in each city.

All of the media key informants had significant experience in advertising/sales/ marketing. Television respondents had on average 14.3 years of experience in their field. The radio and newspaper informants had on average 12.5 and 19.0 years of experience, respectively. Six of the key informants were male and four were female. Eight were Hispanic and two were non-Hispanic Whites. One of the key informants was an immigrant.

Consular Personnel
Interviews with key personnel at Mexican consulates in El Paso, Dallas, Houston, Chicago, New York (Massachusetts is in the New York jurisdiction), and Charlotte, NC were sought in order to obtain information about employer recruitment of Hispanic labor abroad. Of the seven interviews solicited, five were successfully completed. All but one of the consular officials were Mexican nationals. On average, they had 9.0 years of experience in the U.S. Four were male and one was female.

Employment Security Commission Personnel
The North Carolina Employment Security Commission (ESC) is an important source of information about labor market trends in the North Carolina and about how employers recruit employees, including Hispanic workers. In order to gain access to local ESC office personnel, the Regional Director was contacted and asked for permission to interview his staff, which he granted. Interviews were conducted with key personnel in four of the North Carolina Employment Security Commission (ESC) offices in the Triangle. These respondents had held their jobs on average for 24.6 years. All four were White. Two were male and two were female.

Temporary Agency Personnel
Prior research identified temporary agencies as often-used employment intermediaries (Capelli 1995; Holzer 1996; Waldinger 1997). Interviews with local ESC personnel confirmed this finding. Several local temporary agencies advertise prominently in the local Spanish-language newspapers. Several ESC respondents also gave referrals to specific temporary agency personnel who, in turn, were interviewed. Five of these temporary agency personnel were contacted for possible

interviews. A letter of introduction was sent out with one or two articles and the consent form. In most cases, the individual had been contacted by telephone before sending out the information and he or she had already agreed to be interviewed.

Employers
Hispanic workers were shown to be distributed throughout all sectors of the North Carolina economy (Johnson, Johnson-Webb & Farrell, 1999; Johnson-Webb & Johnson, 1996). However, during the 1990s, Hispanics became most visible on construction sites and in service occupations and such "back of the house" jobs as restaurant and hotel cooks and housekeepers in the Triangle. Most previous research and media accounts of the growing presence of Hispanics centers on the role of the construction trades and meat- and poultry-processing (Griffith 1990; Griffith and Runsten 1992; Broadway 1995; Grey 1995; Stull, Broadway et al. 1995; Cooper 1997; Cravey 1997; Cohen 1998; Waldrop 2001; Carter 2002). Therefore, because it had not been widely studied in North Carolina, the hospitality industry was considered a good sector in which to conduct interviews with employers for this study.

Local hospitality industry employers were selected through several means. Those who advertised in North Carolina Spanish-language newspapers were targeted for interviews. Community contacts were also utilized to gain an entrée into several local establishments. Some respondents also gave referrals to others who might be interested in participating. Of thirteen interviews solicited from North Carolina hospitality sector employers, seven were completed. These employers had on average 7.9 years of experience in the hospitality industry. In terms of race and ethnicity, three of these individuals were White (non-Hispanic), three were Hispanic, and one was Black. Three were male and four were female and two of the seven respondents were foreign-born.

The Qualitative Corporate Interview
The interviews for this study were conducted using the qualitative corporate interview strategy —a methodology that has been used by urban and economic geographers (Schoenberger 1989; Schoenberger 1990; Schoenberger 1991; Tyner 1996; McDowell 1997).

Schoenberger (1989) argues that the qualitative corporate interview method is especially appropriate during periods of rapid economic and social transformations that challenge traditional analytical categories and theoretical principles. This method, therefore, was deemed particularly suited for the current research context, which has been characterized by striking economic and demographic change over the 25 years. The qualitative corporate interview consists of an unstandardized format designed to uncover the complex processes or rationales that undergird spatial patterns or specific observed behaviors (e.g., Hispanic labor recruitment). By creating an interview format that allows or gives respondents the leeway to engage in discussions about their specific experiences, the resulting data can provide a deeper understanding of the perceptions, attitudes, intentions, and motives that can be missed in closed-ended or forced-response surveys.

For the purpose of this research, information was gleaned from the research reviewed in Chapter 2 to create a list of open-ended questions designed to stimulate discussion on a variety of topics relating to Hispanic migration and labor recruitment in the Triangle. Topics covered included: informants' job descriptions and experience in the labor market, observed changes in the labor market in recent years, effect of the chronic labor shortage, respondents' experiences with Hispanic workers, their attitudes about their Hispanic workers and native-born workers, modes of recruitment and retention, geographical areas of recruitment, the ethnic, race and gender makeup of their workforces (as well as any other information they wanted to offer about their Hispanic workers), and documentation status of their Hispanic employees.

Typically, the key informant interviews were begun by asking one or two general questions about the growing presence of Hispanics in the Triangle. However, most of the interviews quickly evolved into wide-ranging discussions that provided a wealth of qualitative data about the strategies employed to recruit Hispanic labor. Copious notes were taken during the telephone interviews with media personnel in the gateway cities. The local interviews were audio tape-recorded and hand-written field notes were compiled for these interviews as well. Both the hand written field notes and the audiotapes were then transcribed into a Word® document for further analysis and evaluation.

The resulting interview data were analyzed using NU DIST®, a qualitative data analysis software package. NU DIST® allows the importation of transcribed interview data as text files, and once imported, the documents can be searched for clues, themes, or nodes of information. NU DIST® greatly enhances the researcher's ability to sift through data in a systematic way. The key informant data were coded into several recurring themes, which are presented in Chapter 7.

CHAPTER 7
Data Analysis and Results

Employer Preferences for Hispanic Labor

Respondents were very frank in discussing their impressions of the local Hispanic labor force. Informants readily described the lengths to which they were willing to go to hire and retain Hispanic workers. In a tight labor market, one might expect that employers would go to extraordinary lengths to recruit or retain any employee. In some cases there was evidence of the willingness to do this. But, as will be shown below, the most extraordinary lengths were often reserved for Hispanic workers. Employers described the ways in which they accommodate their Hispanic employees. Triangle employers were so willing to accommodate their Hispanic workers because of their deeply held conviction that Hispanic workers, most notably Mexicans, have an excellent work ethic.

This notion of work ethic is problematic. While employers were enthusiastic about the loyalty, disciplined efforts and reliability of their Hispanic workers, much about their other qualities and characteristics went unmentioned. Part of the perception of Hispanics as good workers may be rooted in the fact that many of these workers are undocumented and are therefore vulnerable to abuses by employers and crew leaders. If they are undocumented, they may be less likely to complain about working conditions, or to seek treatment or compensation if injured on the job. Thus, the vulnerability of the undocumented Hispanic workforce might translate into material savings and this would enhance the value of the Hispanic worker to the employer. The fact that North Carolina is a right to work state and therefore has no strong tradition of labor organizing further reinforces the vulnerability of the undocumented Hispanic working population. Therefore the term "work ethic," as used by respondents, may be a euphemism for a compliant, vulnerable work force.

The interviews revealed that employers perceive Hispanics to be hard workers. This attitude did not seem to vary by the race or ethnicity of the employer.

> ...the Mexican will not...they will not talk, while they're working, to each other. Now, when they take a break... they'll talk and laugh at lunchtime, they'll laugh and tell jokes and everything and [then], back to work...I work with them on the weekends at my farm and, you know you have a hard time getting them to even stop and take a break. Well the employer likes that, I mean...you know it's so different than...[American workers] leaning on the shovel handle going down the highway. You don't see a Mexican leaning on a shovel handle. Mexican'll sit there and use that shovel to smooth up or pick up or doing something while he's waiting there...an American'll sit there and lean on the shovel handle. –Key informant[13]

One respondent shared the following view

> Well...with...the people coming up from Mexico, they're definitely coming up here to work and...sometimes... employers are, have been frustrated with American workers period...Or sometimes it's not that...they've given up on American workers, but they, well, they don't have enough of them and...Mexican workers have the reputation of ...being...reliable, more reliably hard working...that's why I say they [Mexican workers] have this reputation. –ESC informant

Another told of his experiences.

> Well, they [Hispanic workers] drive all the way from Benson and Fayetteville. They come from St. Pauls, which is about two hours from here. They come from everywhere. They actually, you know...the good thing about the Hispanic workers is they're coming, and they'll work at anything and they will work hard. *They will work hard.* I mean that is one of the things that

have impressed...the employers, here in NC. That this group who actually, I mean they will work... And will drive regardless of...where they actually stay at. I mean they will drive if they have to two hours. And then, you know, and they will work. *I mean they will work.* –Triangle employer

The interviews were replete with anecdotes and opinions of this type. Several employers, however, did not stereotype Hispanics, but recognized that there are problems with all workers.

You know, and I'm not always right [that Hispanics are the best workers]. I mean I've had problems...I just fired a guy who had worked for me for several years, who's Mexican, because he's had, he has a drinking problem and he's had one all along and there's been occasional problems every now and then. But he had a real...a family crisis that happened recently and I tried to work with him on it but he was aware of how I felt about it, we talked about it, I gave him another chance and he went on a drunk. 'Cause he's not happy with what's going on in his life right now...And I'm sorry. It was a 3-day drunk. You don't have a job. And I mean you finally, I mean...lots of employers would have fired him the first time around...and I, I said no. You can't come back. And actually he's a pretty decent worker. If he goes back to Mexico gets his family, you know, comes back here a year from now, I would probably rehire him. - Triangle employer

Even with the problems associated with this employee, this employer still maintained an attitude of accommodation. This willingness to accommodate Hispanic workers among the Triangle employers who were interviewed for this study was quite common, as will be shown below.

I came here to NC, where there's more jobs than what there is people in here and they're [native-born workers] still not working...I got people who that you know, well I'm not gonna say...Americans or Hispanics 'cause I have both. But I got employees that have come to my office, worked for a day and quit. Why? No reason why. They either, you call them up at

> the house, and...they sleeping. "Hey what happened? You didn't go to work?" "Oh, I was sleeping. Uh, I couldn't get up." Or either sick..."Why didn't you call?" "Oh, I forgot."
> –Temporary agency recruiter[14]

Several employers did not consider an excellent work ethic to be just a Hispanic trait, but commented upon how immigrants in general have an exemplary work ethic.

> ...in conversations I've been exposed to [with other employers] and then comments through magazine articles, our literature for my industry [human resources]...I get a feeling that...my opinion would say that they [employers] view the ...employment workforce from abroad, whether it be Southeast Asia, the Middle East or Latin countries [to be better workers]...-Triangle employer

One respondent recounted her experiences in the following way

> They [immigrant workers] are so appreciative of the opportunity. They're appreciative of the money...they work like Trojans. But you know, I think it goes without saying, when you haven't had, and all of a sudden you have an opportunity, you are very appreciative...we used to, at one time, have a huge population of Vietnamese who worked for us. When the Vietnamese first started coming in back in the '80s. And let me tell you something, those people...I started off with one...I ended up with over a hundred and fifty working for me. So that's what I'm saying. Word of mouth and they come through...if [the employer] wanted them to work 7 days a week, they were there. If they wanted them to work 12 hours a day, they did. And they appreciate it, they didn't call out, they went to work and if they were complaining it was in Vietnamese and none of us knew what the hell they were saying! But it was so much...better than what they had left behind and they were so appreciative that...[one Vietnamese worker wrote her a letter every month]...Thanking me for getting him that job. And he wrote me letters about how the money that he had made helped rescue the rest of his family who were the Boat People...and that's what I'm saying, the

appreciation factor is so high...and that's exactly why these Hispanic folks work as hard. –Temporary agency recruiter

In describing the virtues of Hispanic workers, employers talked of the wider problem of the lack of a work ethic among American workers in general and youth in particular.

...so I think the whole...American work ethic, that...I had, that my mother had, that your grandmother had, your mother, we're losing that. With each generation that's coming along it's dwindling...you know, these people, these young folks today, you know, they don't want to be given direct orders. They want you to explain everything as to why!...But they really question authority. I mean, not only the 17-year-olds...the 25-year-olds, they really question authority. And want to understand it clearly before they buy into it. –Temporary agency recruiter

Occasionally, remarks of this type had a race-based discriminatory cast to them.

I think it's a mindset...I see 'em come in. You know, they have $50 nails, they have $50 hairdos, they have cell phones, they have pagers. And you know, they're on welfare! Now, I sit here, and do I become angry? Yes I'm angry! I'm really angry...not that I think that they shouldn't have those things. But, I think that they should have those things the same way I would have those things and that's by getting your ass up and going to work! Excuse my...I mean this is going to sound terrible!-Temporary agency recruiter[15]

However, mostly these attitudes transcended race, at least for American workers.

...and so most of my kitchen staff was Caucasian twenty-somethings. And they drove me nuts. And I still have a few of them and I have a couple of them that are...that have been really good workers, but in general...I can see my prejudice is coming out. They never learned how to work. I mean, I learned how to work when I was kid. My mother had me standing on a footstool washing dishes and drying silverware and ironing my dad's handkerchiefs, you know, before I could even, before I even went to school...And these kids don't know how to work. And therefore they get in a situation, it's hot and dirty. That kitchen, even with an air conditioner in the back in the middle of the summer, you know, can be over a hundred [degrees]...I mean, I even like some of these kids... They're real nice kids... and you wish them well...it's a different thing in terms of attitude about work...I mean you know there's, a much higher rate of tardiness with the Caucasian twenty-somethings than I [have] with the Mexicans. You know, the schedule says 9:30...they're [Mexican workers] here at 9:30 or they're here at 9:20...if they ride the bus...they find out the bus that makes sure to get them on time. The white kids you know, go, "well you know I could either be half hour...earlier or I could be 15 minutes late." Of course, [they're] going to be 15 minutes late every time. And [their] excuse is "well that's when the bus comes." And you know the thing is, I don't fire people for things like that, I'm a pretty lenient employer because...the next kid that I hire is not gonna have any different attitude. They are gonna have the same attitude and I'm gonna have to start from scratch. And they might be worse! –Triangle employer[16]

Therefore, work ethic is a very important issue with the employers interviewed for this study. Hispanic workers, and immigrant workers more generally, were viewed to be harder workers with better attitudes toward work than were native-born workers. This perception might give Hispanic workers in the Triangle an incredible advantage in the work force. And this perception is why these employers are so willing to accommodate them in the various ways documented below.

Formal Recruitment Strategies

Newspaper Advertising
Prior research confirmed that newspaper advertising has long been a popular and effective method of labor recruitment (Waldinger, 1997; Holzer, 1996; Capelli, 1995). To determine if newspaper advertising in distant communities played a major role in Hispanic labor recruitment

to North Carolina, the classified advertisement sections of the major English-language newspapers in six cities, which served as major points of origin for Hispanics who moved to North Carolina, were reviewed. Therefore, a comprehensive review and evaluation of the classified ads appearing in the Sunday editions of these six newspapers during the months of June and November in 1980, 1988, and 1996, served as the basis for the analysis that follows.

Altogether, more than 66,000 advertisements were reviewed. As Table 7-1A shows, only 1% (n = 739) of the advertisements surveyed were placed by out-of-state employers. This suggests that advertising was not a major method of labor recruitment during the study period. However, looking across the three sample periods, out-of-state advertising was more common in 1988 than it was in 1980 and 1996. Whereas total advertising was more evenly distributed across the three time periods, of the advertisements surveyed, the largest proportion of out-of-state advertisements (1.8%) was found the 1988 sample of newspapers. Moreover, over half of this out-of-state advertising appeared in newspapers published in Texas, a state with a very large Hispanic population and which is an immigrant gateway.

Notwithstanding the overall low rates of out-of-state advertising, Tables 7-1B and 7-1C reveal the extent to which employers in the Southeast (South Atlantic Division) generally, and in North Carolina particularly, may have engaged in out-of-state advertising. This analysis was deemed important because in contrast to the rest of the nation, this was the region that experienced the most rapid economic growth, and thus the greatest demand for labor during the 1980s and 1990s.

As Table 7-1B shows, one-third of the out-of-state advertisements identified via the content analysis were placed by employers based in the Southeast. Paralleling the temporal pattern uncovered in the analysis of the total sample of advertisements, the highest percentage of out-of-state advertisements placed by employers in the Southeast was in the 1988 sample, after the passage of the amnesty legislation (IRCA, 1986) two years earlier. Also, similar to the data for all out-of-state advertisements, employers from the Southeast tended to advertise in Texas papers.

North Carolina-based employers contributed just 3.2% of the out-of-state advertisements identified in the content analysis of the major English-language newspapers. This percentage did not vary

Table 7-1. Distribution of Advertisements* by Geographical Location, Time Period and Newspaper

A. Percent of the Total Sample of Advertisements that were from Out of State

	Total # of Ads in the Sample	Total # of Out of State Ads	% that were Out of State
1980	22,789	173	0.8%%
1990	20,091	366	1.8%%
1996	23,140	200	0.9%%
Total Sample	66,020	739	1.1%%

B. Percent of Out of State Advertisements that were from the Southeast and North Carolina

	Total # of Out of State Ads	% from SE	% from NC
1980	173	27.2%	3.5%
1990	366	39.9%	3.0%
1996	200	27.5%	3.5%
Total Sample	739	33.6%	3.2%

Source: **Boston Globe; New York times; Chicago Tribune; El Paso Times; Dallas Morning News; Houston Chronicle*; employment advertisements in sampled issues, 1980, 1990 and 1996.

Table 7-1 (cont.). Distribution of Advertisements* by Geographical Location, Time Period and Newspaper

C. Percent of Advertisements by Newspaper

	Total # of Out of State Ads	% Boston Globe	% NYT	% TX Papers	% Chicago Tribune
1980	173	20.8%	7.5%	50.9%	11.6%
1990	366	7.9%	6.0%	68.9%	15.3%
1996	200	1.5%	9.5%	44.0%	32.0%
Total Sample	739	11.9%	7.3%	57.8%	18.9%

D. Percent of Out of State Advertisements that were from the Southeast by Newspaper

	Total # of Ads from the SE	% Boston Globe	% NYT	% TX Papers	% Chicago Tribune
1980	47	10.6%	21.3%	36.2%	8.5%
1990	146	3.4%	6.2%	68.5%	11.6%
1996	55	5.5%	14.5%	40.0%	27.3%
Total Sample	248	5.2%	10.9%	56.0%	14.5%

Source: *Boston Globe; New York times; Chicago Tribune; El Paso Times; Dallas Morning News; Houston Chronicle; employment advertisements in sampled issues, 1980, 1990 and 1996.

Table 7-1 (cont.). Distribution of Advertisements* by Geographical Location, Time Period and Newspaper

E. Percent of Out of State Advertisements that were from the North Carolina by Newspaper

	Total # of Ads from the NC	% Boston Globe	% NYT	% TX Papers	% Chicago Tribune
1980	6	33.3%	0.0%	66.7%	0.0%
1990	11	0.0%	0.0%	72.7%	27.3%
1996	7	0.0%	14.3%	57.1%	28.6%
Total	24	8.3%	4.2%	62.5%	20.8%

Source: *Boston Globe; New York times; Chicago Tribune; El Paso Times; Dallas Morning News; Houston Chronicle*; employment advertisements in sampled issues, 1980, 1990 and 1996.

substantially from one sample period to the next. However, not unlike their counterparts in other states in the Southeast, Texas newspapers were the favored advertising venue for North Carolina employers. Almost two-thirds of the North Carolina-based out-of-state advertisements identified appeared in Texas newspapers (mainly the Dallas Morning News).

What kinds of jobs were out-of-state employers advertising for in the sampled newspapers? For all of the out-of-state advertisements identified, one-half sought to fill jobs in manufacturing and other transformative activities (Table 7-2A). Nearly all of the remaining advertisements were for personal services employment opportunities (38.4%). Basically, the same pattern holds for employers in the southeast U.S. who engaged in out-of-state advertising during the study periods (Table7-2B. However, advertisements from North Carolina employers, though small in number, did not conform to this pattern. As Table 7-2C shows, close to 71% of the out-of-state advertisements were for transformative activities and 25% were for jobs in personal services. Over time, however, there was a steady increase in the percentage of personal services employment advertisements, from 0.0% in 1980, to 22% in 1988, to 44% in 1996. These data are consistent with the overall trend in labor demand in the North Carolina economy during

Table 7-2. Distribution of Advertisements* by Geographical Location, Time Period and Job Classification

A. Percent of the Total Sample of Advertisements that were from Out of State

	Total # of Out of State Ads	% Primary	% Transformative	% Personal Services
1980	173	4.6%	59.5%	28.6%
1990	366	1.1%	53.6%	39.6%
1996	200	1.5%	52.0%	44.5%
Total Sample	739	2.0%	54.5%	38.4%

B. Percent of the Out of State Advertisements that were from the Southeastern U.S.

	Total # of Ads from the SE	% Primary	% Transformative	% Personal Services
1980	39	5.1%	71.8%	23.1%
1990	130	1.5%	52.3%	46.2%
1996	48	0.0%	54.2%	45.8%
Total Sample	217	1.8%	56.2%	41.9%

C. Percent of the Total Sample of Advertisements that were from North Carolina

	Total # of Ads from the NC	% Primary	% Transformative	% Personal Services
1980	6	0.0%	100.0%	0.0%
1990	9	11.1%	66.7%	22.2%
1996	9	0.0%	55.6%	44.4%
Total	24	4.2%	70.8%	25.0%

Source: *Boston globe; New York times; Chicago Tribune; El Paso Times; Dallas Morning News; Houston Chronicle*; employment advertisements in sampled issues, 1980, 1990 and 1996.

the study period. As more high technology and business and professional services jobs developed in the Triangle, there was a concomitant demand for personal services workers.

Figure 7-1. Advertisements Placed by NC Employers in Selected Newspapers[17]

Houston Chronicle, June 16, 1988

ALBANILES Especializados. En Teja, No Se Necesita. Experiencia. Prueba De Permiso De Tradajo Y Numero De Seguro Social. Llamar 305-488-1671. Despues de las 5. Por hora $6.50

Houston Chronicle, November 16, 1988

CAR WASH HELP Wanted in Charlotte NC, Louisville KY, Cincinnati OH. We are looking for hard workers who see themselves as winners. Top performance can earn up to $15,000/year. Se Habla Espanol (*sic*). Interviews will be held in Houston on Nov. 8 & 9. Call Tom Krell at 704-537-3700 to arrange for interview.

El Paso Times, June 1, 1980

TILESETTERS Needed. Must know mud work. Residential & commercial jobs. Must be eligible to relocate to Riley (*sic*), N. Carolina. Call collect 919-859-5820

Dallas Morning News, November 26, 1988

FAMILY to help on dairy farm (Mexican preferred). Must run machinery. Call 919-366-4806 after 8 p.m.

That North Carolina-based employers did target Hispanic workers in their out-of-state advertising is clearly shown in Figure 7-1. Several of the advertisements found appear to be directly targeted at Hispanic workers. One of these advertisements lists a Charlotte, NC area code and is in Spanish. It is for bricklayers, a skilled trade. Several of them mention "crew leaders" and "crews," which are code words for Hispanic labor. One is an advertisement for workers for car washers in Kentucky, Ohio, and North Carolina, which states, "*se habla español*" ("we speak Spanish"). Noted, also, is that this employer was willing to hold interviews in Houston, TX (Figure 7-1). Another is an advertisement for a family to help on a dairy farm in eastern North Carolina, which explicitly states, "Mexican preferred."

Data Analysis and Results

Although the propensity was low and mostly concentrated in the late 1980s, the foregoing results of the content analysis revealed that North Carolina-based employers did advertise for Hispanic workers in mainstream English-language newspapers in traditional immigrant gateway communities. None of the Spanish-language newspaper personnel interviewed in this research, however, recalled receiving any out-of-state advertisements from North Carolina-based employers. Nor did any of them report taking advertisements from employers from any other state in the southeast region.

Several of the informants who worked at Spanish-language newspapers in the points of origin indicated that most of their out-of-state advertisements originated in nearby states (i.e. within commuting distance) such as Wisconsin (Chicago) and New Jersey (New York). One informant in Houston noted that most out-of-state employers do not consider advertising in Spanish-language newspapers there because most of the English-language newspapers (e.g. the Houston Chronicle) now have "some Spanish format."

North Carolina employers and employment intermediaries generally viewed local Spanish-language newspaper advertising to be the most important formal mode of recruiting Hispanic labor. One local fast food employer remarked that advertising in the *Las Paginas de Trabajos* [The Spanish Job Pages], a free newspaper that is distributed in the Triangle, was a very effective way to recruit Hispanic workers. Local temporary agencies also utilize the local Spanish-language newspapers to recruit Hispanic workers, as the following quote illustrates.

> ...we have targeted Hispanic employees in the *Hispanic Job Pages*...at the times when we've done that, I don't think we've ever been prepared enough for the amount of individuals that come looking for employment.-Triangle employer

This informant said that he began advertising in the *Hispanic Job Pages* after the newspaper solicited an advertisement from him. Other local employers reported that they advertised in Spanish-language newspapers in other North Carolina cities. For example, a food service employer in the Triangle noted that she had advertised in a Greensboro-based Spanish-language newspaper.

Radio and Television Advertising

Radio and television advertising personnel who were interviewed in the gateway cities did not view their media as particularly important in terms of out-of-state labor recruitment. However, the majority of out-of-state radio advertising personnel interviewed reported that their stations did broadcast job advertisements from local employers on a regular basis. Spanish-language television personnel stated that TV advertising was cost prohibitive, especially in comparison to less costly newspaper and radio advertising, and thus, they could not compete in the advertising market.

In the past, according to one informant, the Employment Security Commission (ESC) advertised area employment opportunities over local television and radio stations in the Triangle area. The informant noted, however, that the ESC's practice of advertising on regular TV ended about twenty years ago. According to another informant, local employers often used cable television commercials to recruit semi-skilled workers to the Triangle from areas within commuting distance.

Job Fairs

Nearly all of the informants interviewed in this research considered job fairs to be an effective, albeit relatively new method of recruiting Hispanic labor - both locally and in distant communities. One informant stated, for example, that the ESC office in which she worked had participated in the job fair at *La Fiesta del Pueblo*, a popular annual Hispanic festival in Chapel Hill. Another commented on job fairs in Sanford, NC.

> ...I never actually had any interest in Sanford until about 5 months ago, I starting seeing this huge amount of people I could say 90% of those were Hispanic [were coming] to our office to apply...And that's when I realized, I mean Wow! There's that many Hispanics in here [Sanford]? So when I came over [to Sanford] to recruit, 'cause I went to recruit just people from here, I mean, sheesh, it was incredible, I didn't know that I had that many...I mean I was driving on the road and you see Hispanics toward here and Hispanics toward there.
> –Triangle employer

This employer noted further that his job fairs, which were advertised in the local Spanish-language newspapers, brought in large numbers of

Hispanic applicants, who in turn, told their friends and relatives about available job opportunities.

H-2A Visa Program

Several informants noted that the H-2A visa program, which is a formal mechanism through which farmers are able to recruit agricultural workers from abroad, has played a key role in the migration and settlement of Hispanics in urban areas of North Carolina. Several ESC respondents described how the H-2A visa program works.

> ...we have job orders for migrant, for farm workers to do this type of work. And what the job orders are is what they call H-2A. What that means is, in order [for employers] to be able to legally bring in foreign workers to do a particular job, you need to establish that there are no indigenous workers to do that type of work...So, you [the employer] write up a job order and you advertise that job order and...you give it to the Employment Security Commission...just really to establish that there are none or insufficient indigenous workers. Then, you can bring in the foreign workers...there are orders in the system now from...the Migrant and Seasonal Farm Workers Association...basically there're very few people, very few indigenous workers placed in these jobs from these orders. These people are brought in from Mexico. -ESC respondent[18]

In addition to the Migrant and Seasonal Farm Workers Association, other informants indicated that the H-2A visa program was widely used by the North Carolina Grower's Association to bring large numbers of Mexicans and smaller numbers of Haitians and Puerto Ricans to the state for temporary agricultural work.

> ...the North Carolina Growers Association has been around for...maybe 10 years or so, I'm not sure... they are... the largest [recruiter], I think, they're bringing in 13,000 [migrant workers] this year [1999], [that is] the highest, I think that's it's ever been. -Key informant

This informant concluded by saying that

...there've got to be other folk doing that...[but] nobody is as organized as what they are...

Another informant described how the recruitment process works.

...employers send recruiters to Mexico to attract workers into the program. The recruiters are by and large Mexican or Mexican American. I have seen a Cuban American recruiter. But most recruiters are someone who can speak Spanish and can relate to the workers. The workers are charged money for their participation in the program. Up to $500 is charged by recruiters in order for a worker to get involved. –Consular official in Texas

Even though workers are documented to do only agricultural work, North Carolina-based informants indicated that when some of these workers find out about jobs in the cities, they leave the farms to pursue employment opportunities there. Informants noted that better working conditions, living conditions, and the rate of pay were considerations in the decisions of these agricultural workers to move to urban areas. According to several respondents, these programs have contributed to observed Hispanic settlement in urban areas of North Carolina.

...The farmers, you know, help 'em get their green card and, and soon as they get their green card they...say "*Adios!*" and head for the city where they can work in air-conditioned buildings and have vacation and lunch hour, things like that. –Key informant

Employment Intermediaries

Consulates
Traditionally, the role or charter of the Mexican consulates is to look after the welfare of the Mexican nationals in their jurisdiction and to provide documents such as *matriculas*, passports, and Mexican voter registration cards. However, Mexican consular officials interviewed in this study indicated that employers in their respective local geographical areas increasingly expect that consulates are a repository of information about Mexican workers.

> ...We are constantly answering questions: "Do you know of anybody? Can we post something? I need a cleaning lady."
> –Consular official in Chicago

Another consular official noted that

> ...There was a chain of [local] restaurants. One of the managers came into the consulate looking for workers. He was an American. He said that wherever he goes, when he sets up a restaurant, he goes to the Mexican consulate in the area to scout for workers. He said, "Mexicans are the best. They will work 12-13 hours, they will work hard for you."-Consular official in Texas

The following response was given when a respondent was asked if she provided Mexican nationals with employment information.

> If I have it- yes. For instance the Census Bureau is recruiting so they brought some job announcements here. There is a radio program as well, and I direct it. If I have an advertisement from a company I say it. –Consular official in Texas

And in response to a question about whether employers contact the consulate for assistance in finding labor, a source familiar with North Carolina indicated that

> ...They want to know basically where they can find more workers, how they can get more workers, and, what they can do to keep their workers, keep the competition from stealing them...And where they can advertise to get workers and how they can get more of them here or can they get some legalized that are already here. Things like that. –Key informant

However, none of the consular officials in distant cities reported fielding inquiries for workers from North Carolina employers or from those in other states.

Employment Security Commission

This employment intermediary is a very important resource for employers seeking workers and for job seekers. The role of the ESC as an employment intermediary was described as follows

> ...we...help employers find applicants for their listings. They let us know what they're looking for in terms of education and experience and we screen based on that. -ESC informant

In the interviews conducted for this study, ESC officials remarked repeatedly about the drastic changes occurring in the Triangle labor market as a consequence of the influx of Hispanic immigrants. One official noted that Hispanics, mostly males, are increasingly availing themselves of the services of the ESC. Several estimated that Hispanic applicants now constitute between 5% and 10% of their total clientele. To accommodate the growing number of Hispanic job seekers, the ESC has had to hire Spanish-speaking interviewers, which, in turn, further increased the flow of Hispanic job seekers through the office. Officials noted that they experienced difficulty in retaining Spanish-speaking interviewers because they are in such high demand in the Triangle.

Although the ESC is federally mandated not to discriminate in selecting applicants, ESC officials reported that local employers have contacted them and specifically requested Mexican or Hispanic workers.

> At times we have calls from employers who are interested in hiring Hispanic workers simply for the purpose of having somebody who speaks the language...But, we can't recruit a particular ethnic group. We have to refer anyone who's qualified for a job...We're federally mandated to do that. –ESC informant

Another respondent said

> ...Mostly employers ask for someone who is bilingual. And federal law to supply the best candidate for the job regardless of race mandates us. So they tell me what they need and I go down the list of qualified applicants. I don't care if their name is Smith or Jones or Gonzales. Now, sometimes you'll get an employer who says, "I don't mind if they're Hispanic or Mexican..." –ESC informant

And a third indicated that

> ...sometimes we get calls... "Send me Mexicans! Not any...I don't want Americans, I want Mexicans!" And of course we're not able to exactly do that, you know. But uh, you know, "They are great workers! I want Mexicans!" – ESC informant

As noted previously, employers' expressed preference for Mexican labor is rooted in their perception of their excellent work ethic.

Temporary Agencies

Partly as a result of the restructuring of the economy and the rise in demand for a flexible workforce, there has been a dramatic rise in the role of temporary agencies or the staffing industry as a labor recruitment intermediary. Temporary agencies were generally viewed by respondents as having a growing role in Hispanic labor recruitment as well. Many local temporary agencies have begun to specifically target Hispanic workers. One local temporary agency, although it served any applicant that came in the door, had a staff of bilingual interviewers. Also, because their interviewers knew where to go to make contact with Hispanic workers, they were often able to recruit them informally, on the spot. Describing one local temporary agency, an informant said

> ...I think all of their people are bilingual, all of their interviewers...and they're very heavily into recruiting of the Mexican workers...I was talking to one of their interviewers and he's was out driving around and he just saw a bunch of a Mexicans at an apartment complex and so he just went out and went to them and, you know, handed them his..."Come on down to our place." He had his flyers with him...-ESC Informant

Informal Methods of Recruitment

Word of Mouth

Respondents also freely discussed the informal methods they used to recruit workers. Although most of the North Carolina respondents extolled the importance of local newspaper advertising, the one method that seemed to hold the overwhelming importance to these employers in terms of recruiting Hispanic workers was word of mouth. This was true for recruiting workers in the local area as well as from abroad. This practice, which is also used extensively to recruit workers in general, is so ingrained that many employers have developed policies within their establishments to better utilize this method as a resource.

Regarding the recruitment of Mexican workers from abroad, one informant had this to say:

> ...most Mexicans find out about jobs in North Carolina urban areas through oral communications from their own people. From their *paisanos* [person from the same country or region], then they bring their families. -Mexican national informant

Another informant said

> I don't know of any active and organized recruitment effort. I think it's mostly by word of mouth. A huge amount of money is sent back home and people talk about the jobs here. –Consular official in New York

Still others viewed the spread of information by word of mouth within the Hispanic community about employment opportunities as a cultural phenomenon.

> It's a cultural thing, an ethnic thing. I'll tell my brother and his brother tells his friend. –Triangle employer

Further elaborating on the cultural theme, another informant said

> I could say that's the number two most successful way of recruiting. Actually networking. It's like I said, once they [Hispanics] feel comfortable with someone, then they will

> communicate out to their friends or their families. And then you will get another whole group just coming in here without advertisement. So, it's all based on how you treat the people...If they feel comfortable with you, if they know that you, in fact, are there to help them out...they are willing to stick with you...So, as long as you treat them...like humans...they will really, you know, they feel comfortable. They know that if they need any help they can just go straight to your office...And they know they'll find the help there. You'll not just get one, you'll get a hundred...-Triangle temporary agency recruiter

Owing to their strong work ethic, one employer noted that she would be far more inclined to rely on word of mouth referrals from her Hispanic workers.

> ...So, you know, if you have a choice between...you've got an opening and...one of my Mexicans says, "well I've got a friend that I'll bring in to meet you" or one of my Caucasians says "well you want to hire my buddy?"...I'm gonna hire the Latino first every time. Every time!-Triangle employer[19]

Informants who were familiar with specific local Hispanic communities reported that *tiendas* or Hispanic markets often double as a place to congregate and share information about employment opportunities and other important issues.

> ...the Mexican has the greatest pipeline in the world. And he knows what the going rate is and that's what he wants. And if you don't pay it, he'll go down the street. So I've not seen any Mexicans that'll work for 3 dollars and hour or 4 dollars or whatever, you know you hear all kinds of stories. The Mexican knows, you know when they get together at their little grocery stores in the evenings and weekends they know, they have a tremendous pipeline. And they talk among themselves and they know where the...what the going rate is and that's what the heck they want. –Key informant

Moreover, most local *tiendas* have a bulletin board where local employers or even someone who is seeking a worker for an odd job can post an advertisement.

Raiding

Owing to the tightness of the local labor market, employers described raiding, or stealing, employees from another establishment as a common practice. Employers were so desperate for good workers that they had no qualms about engaging in this practice. However, this tactic appeared to have been used by these employers only in the recruitment of Hispanics.

> ...you look at restaurants, because of the demand and lack of American workers...many Hispanics that used to be in agriculture are now going to these other trades...in terms of both skilled and unskilled, I think construction work competes so tough, we've gotten reports where, we talked to one foreman, who went to lunch, came back and his whole crew was gone. Another contractor come by, offered them more money and took the whole crew. –ESC informant

He went on to say that the practice is also common in the retail sector.

> ...also in, in retail, restaurants a couple retail managers have told me that when they go somewhere for some personal business anytime and they deal with an employee that's really good they, they'll make them an offer on the spot. You know, what are you making, now? I'll up that, X-number of cents or dollars. So there is some, whether it's conscious raiding or not, but it's raiding nonetheless. –ESC informant

One Hispanic fast food restaurant employer vividly described an instance of raiding.

> I was at one of the restaurants and I saw three guys [Hispanics] who were wearing a competitor's uniform. They were at the bus stop in front of my store waiting on the bus. So I went up to them and asked them how they were doing [in Spanish] and introduced myself. I asked them if they wanted to come work for me. They asked how much more will you pay? I asked

> them to consider that if they worked for me, they'd be right here, they wouldn't have to ride the bus to work. They tried to ask me for more money, but I was able to convince them that the time saved would be worth it. We could see about a raise later. But the one condition was that I had to hire all three of them on the spot.-Triangle employer[16]

Other Informal Methods

Anecdotal evidence exists that recruiting of Hispanic workers for non-agricultural work does occur in Mexico.

> I don't have any personal knowledge, but I hear from a reliable source that there are recruiting posters on the border. They hear about jobs and they cross over.- Chatham County respondent

This was also confirmed by a personal source unrelated to this study. However, none of the Mexican consular personnel interviewed reported ever seeing billboards or signs at the border advertising jobs in North Carolina.

One aspect of informal recruitment that was touched on in the interviews is the fact that some employers reported sharing information with one another to facilitate the recruitment of Hispanic workers. Two respondents reported using networks they had with other employers to recruit Hispanic workers, or to find jobs for relatives of their current Hispanic employees. One employer described how she and another employer cooperated in helping Hispanic workers to find employment.

> ...[a local butcher] also has Hispanics in this area...and he might be a person for you to talk to...and...he had some, how did we do this? We share some employees as well. And I can't remember exactly how we got the connection to begin with but...there was a point when somebody, I...think this woman knew that he hired Hispanics, so she called him and then he called me. But anyway, it was a woman who is a house manager for one of the sororities...And she was looking for a cleaning lady...And between [the butcher] and me and talking to my workers, we found her...a Mexican woman to, to take the job. So, you know, in my experience, I would say that we [local employers in her area] work together...

These informal recruitment networks can be very closed. In this instance, an employer decided she wanted to hire a Hispanic and knew the exact network in which to look for one, with no need of formal advertising or screening. These types of recruitment strategies may have detrimental impacts on members of other race or ethnic groups who do not have access to such networks.

Accommodation Strategies

Employers reported a variety of ways in which they accommodated their Hispanic employees. Many of these methods were often reserved only for Hispanic workers and were not offered to or even considered for native-born workers. The most common accommodations mentioned by employers were those that helped them to cope with the language barrier. The translation of employment or work related materials into Spanish was an often-used accommodation.

> I think around 1986 things started to be translated at the local level, just a very few things. As far as the ESC, there are not a lot of things translated, not a lot of Spanish materials. –ESC respondent

The time frame for when the ESC started translating these materials coincides with the IRCA of 1986 (amnesty).

Several of the employers interviewed offered English as a Second Language (ESL) classes as an incentive to keep their Hispanic workers. Some went so far as to hold these classes on the premises, immediately after shifts ended. Other employers, in order to encourage their employees to learn English, offered to pay for the ESL classes and would give employees time off to attend them.

Informants at the ESC and at local temporary agencies reported that they used Spanish-speaking interviewers in their offices to assist Hispanic applicants. Those ESC offices that did not have a translator at the time of the interview were actively seeking a replacement. Employers grappled with this issue by increasing their efforts to hire bilingual staff or managers. In fact, several of the food service employers interviewed were pushing hard to train or prepare Spanish-speaking workers for hourly or salaried management positions.

One would expect that the language barrier would be an almost insurmountable one. Employers did view it as somewhat of an

Data Analysis and Results

inconvenience, but, as the following quote illustrates, they had developed other innovative ways to deal with it.

> ...my assistant [manager]...he is extremely positive toward Hispanics...As am I, and we both speak a little bit of Spanish. He speaks more than I do. He's real interested...as a matter of fact he's going to Mexico for a semester to study...so you know, it's very clear to them [the Hispanic employees] that we like them. –Triangle employer

Another respondent recounted one of the means that employers use to overcome the language and cultural barriers.

> ...I think on the whole that employers are becoming more sensitive. You know, if you talk to Wake Tech or the community colleges... apparently there've been new courses on supervising different...on different cultures...And there are some courses on strictly...the Hispanic, that you don't get too close, you don't put your hand on... and some of the no-nos that's commonly accepted here [in the US] but yet to the Hispanic is an offense...-ESC informant

Other informants described similar approaches.

> I used to live in Chatham County and I got a bulletin from that community college there...Central Carolina Technical College, I believe. And in this...catalogue...it offered English as a Second Language, and the classes were actually given at the Golden Poultry Plant...And, Spanish for Supervisors or something and that was also given at the, at the plant. So...to make this thing work and it seems to work quite well...the accommodations have been made...-ESC informant

Another informant said

> ...there've been a lot of things done in the county to accommodate...those who don't speak English...again it's, it's a matter of opinion and what you're bottom line is. ...person A needs a chicken gutted. Could care less whether you speak

English, if you can gut that chicken. Person B needs you to program and calibrate to umpteen thousandths tolerance some kind of metal machine and then they might care if you understand that or not (laughs)... so you know, you've got both happening. –ESC informant[20]

Employers described another method they often used to compensate for the language barrier: using existing Hispanic workers to train and acclimate new hires. Describing a situation in which a Hispanic worker was leaving the work site, one employer indicated that before they leave they will say

"...Oh but my brother will come." You know, and if you're really lucky they'll bring their brother or their cousin for a week before they leave and get 'em kinda semi-trained, learn the ropes, do...help with the language barrier that sort of thing. –Triangle employer

One ESC office developed a resourceful way to better serve its Spanish-speaking applicants, which was described in the following way.

...We had an interviewer that is no longer here, we were sorry to lose him. He knew a native Spanish-speaker and he developed...with this person...a [cassette] tape where he would play the tape and the tape would ask the person the questions that we needed to know so we could...do the application...you know, what is your address? And what is your...your work history and the type of work that you want and this was quite helpful. –ESC informant

Hispanic employers often ran interference for their Hispanic employees. Several employers remarked about cultural miscommunications. Hispanic employees, although exemplifying a good work ethic, may get their feelings trampled on by an insensitive or ignorant employer.

...now let's look at the Hispanic workforce in general. They're usually more loyal, and they are usually more dedicated...I always see the same thing, loyal, dedicated as well as also, a hard worker. Normally. Normally...so as that's...I would say an attribute, a bonus. But at the same time it can also hurt. Especially when there is a miscommunication...-Triangle employer[21]

Elaborating on the miscommunication problem, another respondent said

I mean, if in fact, if they feel that somebody is taking advantage of them, then yeah, you can believe me, they will get upset, whether they can communicate or not. What they will do is they will just leave the job...They will not even say anything. They will just leave...OK? They will not even say, "Look, I'm quitting." Or anything. Or they won't tell you the reason why they just leave. –Triangle employer

A temporary agency employer, who places large numbers of Hispanics in jobs in the Triangle area, described how he dealt with problems that might arise between his Hispanic workers and the contractor in the following manner.

I got bilingual people that work on those sites. Which means that if there's a problem in the place, I already have someone up there who takes care of it. And [it] does not even require for me to go out there. -Temporary agency recruiter

One unique accommodation that employers reported was holding a job for an employee who returned to Mexico for his or her annual visit of two to three months. Employers seemed to take these leaves in stride. The employer's experience described below, was very typical of what many others reported.

...I should say it's common for some of the Mexicans in the work force as well as maybe, anyone from Central America. It's common for a portion of them to say, "it's the holidays. I'm going to leave for about 2 1/2 months. I'll be back." You know, and they do come back. [they will say] "I'm going to go home and visit my family." 'Cause a lot of times they still have children back home... usually their parents or...brothers and sisters and relatives that still live at home...you know they send money home, continuously ...throughout the year, but

> they also save up money to go home and have like a good holiday fest with their family and then they return to work.
> –Triangle employer

In response to a question regarding why employers accommodate such leaves, the respondent said

> ... because of the work ethic that they've [the employer] seen. I mean you really, when the year is going pretty well and then they want to take off from June to August for the summer. Or they want to from the early part of December to the early part of February, yeah. You don't want to lose them. That's, I'd say, a common line I hear, you know...I don't want to lose them and...if I got to deal with them being gone for 2 months, I'd rather do that and have them come back.-Triangle employer

ESC informants described another way of accommodating or assisting Hispanic applicants. The local offices often sought assistance from and shared information with social service agencies or community groups. One ESC interviewee reported regularly calling upon a local Hispanic community organization for help translating to Hispanic applicants. He also reported telling these organizations about job openings or finding jobs for applicants referred by these organizations.

Sources familiar with the Hispanic population in North Carolina and employers were often reluctant to comment candidly on the documentation status of North Carolina Hispanics in general or their employees specifically. Every employer interviewed reported that their employees had documents allowing them to work in the U.S. However, some employers scrutinized documents rigorously while others did not. All of the employers acknowledged that a thriving black market for documents exists in North Carolina. Minimal or cursory scrutiny of documents could be construed as accommodating undocumented Hispanic employees.

> ...And I don't know if you're gonna ask this or not...all of my Hispanics have papers...They are on payroll, they get checks.-Triangle employer

> ...I don't know anything about checking them...So I'm not telling you that their documents aren't forged...But they have

> them and they match...You know, they come to me and they fill out their paper work and they have a Social Security card and they have an alien card, and you know, sometimes some other form of identification. And they all...match. So, that is not a problem in my...I hear that it is...I'm somewhat involved in a Hispanic task force for Orange County. And when I talk to other people in social service agencies that deal with health care and day care and that sort of thing, is that apparently, a lot of, there are a lot of undocumented workers in this area, but I have not, I have had the good fortune of not having to...- Triangle employer

Another respondent answered inquiries about employee documentation status in this way. Laughing, he said

> Well...That's a...that's a really touchy...it's like INS has said...we can't blame...you know, we can't actually not blame, but we can't penalize or do anything to the employer because we are not a INS [Immigration and Naturalization Service]. We go by the law...You show me something, you show me the documents...if look at it and to me...they look...real...And I will take it. According to the laws that the INS has established....Now, it's not my job and of course, I don't have that expertise [to know if documents are authentic] that the INS has...to, in fact, know who is illegal or not...So, it's a big issue. It's a huge issue. -Temporary agency recruiter[22]

A temporary agency employer recounted her experience in dealing with construction contractors who hired undocumented workers. She described a situation in which it was obvious that the Hispanic worker's documentation papers were fraudulent.

> ...what these contractors do, they're not, they don't care about details. They take the license and Social Security card and go Xerox it, they throw it in the pile. For their INS. For their I-9 requirement. Now. If you look at it, you can clearly tell. That one and one are not agreeing...but a lot of people are not doing it and a lot of people don't want to do it because...they don't want to know the truth. -Temporary agency recruiter

She went on to say

> I mean, you know, let's get down to brass tacks...they'll find people who'll pay them under the table...that happens a lot...and I mean, it really is very tragic. And like this guy I'm trying to help now, you know, I really feel bad for him. I would love to help him. But you know I'm limited in terms of what I...his Social Security number doesn't even exist. I mean it's an invalid number...Now, not all of them are invalid. A lot of them are valid numbers, however, they belong to other people. You know, one guy had one and the number he was using, the man died in 1969...but that number's being re-circulated...or they've picked it up somewhere and they've printed it on a card. Now you know the only people, in my opinion, that are profiteering off these people, are the people, if they're coming in out of Texas, that are selling these folks documentations. And I would love to know what they are buying, paying for 'em, I would say anywhere from two to five hundred dollars, probably... for Social Security or IDs or whatever. And even false resident aliens cards, we've seen...and I think that's the unfortunate part...because they're [the scam artists to the undocumented immigrant] saying, "OK, alright you're ready to go. You're legal, here you go." And you aren't legal. And, no here you don't go. –Temporary agency employer

Employers and intermediaries reported that they accommodated Hispanic applicants in groups although they were supposed to screen applicants individually.

> ...And that's one thing about the...Hispanic workers...you hire them in groups. Or they want to be hired in groups and usually the employers are willing to, there's enough openings that they're willing to do that....-ESC informant

The respondent went on to say that

> ...we had an interviewer who was a Spanish-speaker, and some of the Hispanics, of course, would end up at his desk and the supervisor was upset because he always had a crowd around

> his desk instead of just you know, it's supposed to be one at a time, you go from the list and it's one at a time. What is, you know, and what is this crowd? And so...you get Hispanics, you get the whole gang there because they, for different reasons you have someone that is sort of an interpreter for ones whose English is non-existent or not as good, and then you have one who is the driver who has the car and the driver's license. And the interpreter may not be the driver, but they all function as you know...it is a work unit. It's not individuals working; it's a work unit. The work unit cannot function without you know everyone involved in it. And so if...any element of that work unit is lost, the whole work unit usually ends up switching [jobs]...You don't lose one person, you lose the whole gang.- ESC informant

Typically, another respondent said

> ...we don't get employers crews of workers or anything like that. But when Hispanics come to this office they never come alone. Or if you get them the job they say "I have a friend" or I ask them if they have a friend. And most times if I send a Hispanic to a job and he gets it this week, next week there are 3 or 4 more there. Poultry [processing] pays well for this county. Although some of it is mechanized it's still manual labor for the most part. It's the same thing done over and over. It's cold, wet work. It's raw meat greasy and it's repetitive.-ESC informant

The tight labor market in the Triangle also puts pressure on employers to provide recruiting bonuses, other benefits, and incentives to Hispanic employees or prospective employees. The prevalence of raiding only increased this pressure. In response, employers have developed several incentives in order to attract new employees or to retain the ones they had. These incentives were in place not only in jobs with harsh working conditions, such as meat- and poultry-processing, but in restaurants, fast food establishments and hotels as well.

One incentive that was mentioned repeatedly was the hiring bonus. If one employee brought in another employee and that employee worked out, or lasted for at least ninety days, the recruiting employee got a bonus of $50 to $100.

> We also do that. We offer bounty hunters...or a bonus...If you bring on a family member or a friend and they work with us for ninety days you receive $50.-Triangle employer

Another respondent described the incentives used by local employers in the poultry-processing industry. She indicated that their incentives had to be very competitive due to the harsh nature of the work and the high turnover due to injuries. She went on to point out that

> ...They have...a regular hire-in pay rate for trainee. Then they have a shift premium, just like anybody else. They pull a shift, quarter, 10, 15, 20, 30, 40 cents more for the night shifts, whatever. They have a non-absent, non-tardy quarter on the hour bonus per pay period... [every] Two weeks. So if you're not absent and not tardy any in the two-week pay period and your rate is 7 dollars, you actually get paid 7 and a quarter and hour. Uh, [if you] stay [a certain] length of time on night shift [you get a] bonus of like a hundred bucks or something, too. They have a, bring us a good employee, you get a hundred dollar hiring incentive thing. And I'm sure that's probably not all, but those are the biggies...-Chatham County respondent

Several of these incentives were also mentioned by hospitality sector employers, especially the hiring and shift bonuses, as well as the leave of absence after a certain period of employment.

Finally, in areas of the Triangle where public transportation was a challenge, several employers reported that transportation was provided for Hispanic workers. For instance, one employer sent vans to pick up Hispanic workers at their apartment complexes in Durham and transported them to work at a local hotel in the Research Triangle Park. Other informants said that employers often provide free bus tickets to their Hispanic workers.

Employers in this study reported very positive attitudes toward their immigrant Hispanic workers. Some of these employers also expressed negative attitudes toward their native-born workers, particularly those who were between the ages of 16 and 25. A variety of recruiting strategies was also reported, some of which were used strictly for recruiting Hispanic immigrant workers.

These results have implications for the employment prospects of low-wage workers in the Triangle region of North Carolina, and more generally for immigration and workforce development policy. These implications are discussed in detail in the following chapter.

CHAPTER 8
Discussion and Conclusions

Discussion
Over the past decade, North Carolina's demographic make-up has changed dramatically, owing principally to the recent immigration and in-migration of Hispanics. Research indicates that these Hispanic newcomers settled initially in the state's major urban communities, especially along U.S. Interstate 85. However, more recently they have begun to settle in exurban and rural communities throughout the state. Through the use of an array of qualitative research methods, this study has examined the recent immigration and in-migration of Hispanics to North Carolina. It has specifically attempted to assess the role of formal and informal labor recruitment strategies used by North Carolina employers in attracting Hispanic newcomers to the state.

Interpretation of Research Findings
Three overarching research questions guided this study. They are stated below as a guide to the interpretation of the study's major findings.

Why did these North Carolina employers recruit Hispanic labor?

The key informant interviews suggested that local hospitality sector employers are aggressively recruiting Hispanic workers because (1) there is a chronic shortage of semi-skilled labor in the Triangle area and, (2) Hispanics are perceived to have a strong work ethic. At the same employers enthusiastically praised the superior work ethic of Hispanics, especially Mexican workers, the majority of those interviewed also expressed disenchantment with native-born workers, particularly those in the 16- to 25-year-old age group. The findings here are consistent with prior research, which found that employers were extremely critical of the attitudes and work orientations of Black workers (Waldinger 1993; Capelli 1995; Holzer 1996; Moss and Tilly 1996; Waldinger 1997). However, they dispute Kirschenman and Neckerman's findings that employers place White workers first in the hiring queue for entry-level positions (Kirschenman and Neckerman 1990). The disenchantment expressed by employers interviewed for this study placed all native-born workers (not solely Black males) at a distinct disadvantage in the Triangle labor market.

Although employers interviewed in this study mentioned having to grapple with the language barrier as part of dealing with Hispanic immigrant labor, they indicated that their work ethic made it worth the trouble. The perceptions that Triangle employers hold of Hispanic workers definitely gives them a competitive edge in the unskilled labor market.

What formal and informal recruitment strategies were utilized to recruit Hispanic labor?

The newspaper content analysis revealed that some Triangle employers had indeed advertised for Hispanic workers in immigrant gateway communities. However, the evidence gathered suggests that this strategy was employed primarily in the late 1980s, when North Carolina's economic boom was taking off. Moreover, the advertising that was found was focused on the state of Texas, which is a major gateway for immigrants from Mexico and was also one of the major points of origin for Hispanic who came to North Carolina between 1985 and 1990. This suggests that employers may have been targeting Hispanics who had benefited from the amnesty legislation, and who were able to take advantage of emerging employment opportunities in transformative activities (e.g., construction and light manufacturing) and personal services in the Triangle.

Regardless of whether employers recruited locally, from other U.S. jurisdictions, or from abroad, the key informant interviews suggest that word of mouth was by far the most important and effective method of recruiting Hispanic labor for these employers. Advertising in local Spanish-language newspapers was the second most effective method of recruiting Hispanic workers. Both employers themselves and temporary agencies advertised in these outlets.

Job fairs that specifically targeted Hispanic workers were described by a majority of the key informants to be an increasingly more important tool for recruiting Hispanic workers. Such events have become popular coincident with the emergence of Hispanic communities on the North Carolina landscape.

Employers also sought to recruit Hispanic labor through a number of employment intermediaries, including Mexican Consulates, the Employment Security Commission, and temporary agencies. Some of these intermediaries attempted to serve both employers and Hispanics looking for work by referring possible applicants, hiring Spanish-speaking interviewers and by translating employment and safety materials into Spanish.

Finally, raiding or stealing employees was identified as a common method of recruiting Hispanic labor amongst this group of employers. This practice reflected the tightness of the local labor market at the time of the study. Employers tried to steal workers from their competitors because there simply were not enough Hispanic workers to fill the burgeoning demand for labor.

What accommodations did North Carolina employers make to retain Hispanic workers?

Employers reported a variety of ways that they tried to accommodate their Hispanic workers and thus reduce the risk of being raided by a competitor. The most frequent accommodation made was to hire Spanish-language interviewers or otherwise attempt to come to grips with the language barrier. Providing on-site English as a Second Language courses and translating pertinent materials into Spanish was often part of this strategy.

Employers frequently mentioned that they allowed extended leaves for Hispanic employees who returned to their country of origin for an annual visit. Again, the superior work ethic of these employees was a powerful incentive for employers to hold their jobs during these relatively long absences.

Many employers accommodated undocumented immigrant Hispanic employees by not carefully scrutinizing their documents. All of these employers stated that their employees had documents, however, some of them implied that these documents quite possibly could be invalid. In addition to the accommodations mentioned above, a range of work-related financial incentives, such as hiring bonuses and shift bonuses, created a welcoming environment for Hispanic workers and encouraged them to tell their relatives and friends about vacancies or employment in the company.

Conclusions

The findings of this study strongly suggest that employer labor recruitment practices have played a major role in Hispanic migration and settlement in the Triangle over the last twenty years. More specifically, the strongly expressed employer preferences for Hispanic workers in an incredibly tight labor market has set into motion a range of formal and informal labor recruitment strategies. These findings conflict with one of the central tenets of dual labor market theory, which posits that low-skilled immigrant workers come only to take advantage of employment opportunities in the booming economy and intend to return to their country origin once they earn a certain amount of money. While the Hispanic newcomers appear to be sending large sums of money back home to relatives, they do not appear to be returning to their country of origin as dual labor market theory posits. Instead, they are establishing roots in North Carolina, transforming communities, establishing their own businesses, and creating a wide array of community-building institutions, while maintaining ties with their foreign community of origin.

But these results also support dual labor market theory and suggest that employer demand for immigrant labor was a fundamental facet of the influx of Hispanic immigrants to the Triangle. Social networks theory is also supported by the finding that these employers made frequent and extensive use of the social networks of their immigrant employees as a hiring tool. Employer demand and thus hiring behavior was shaped by the tightness of the local labor market, and the chronic shortage of entry-level hospitality workers.

In all likelihood, these communities and the institutions that comprise them will continue to act as migration magnets, attracting a continuous flow of Hispanics into the state. The findings here suggest that the Hispanic newcomers are having a profound impact on the North Carolina communities in which they are settling.

Policy Implications of the Research Findings

One of the most striking results of this study was the connection between employers' demand for labor and the lengths they were willing to go to hire and keep Hispanic workers. This has implications for other workers who are systematically excluded from immigrant job information networks. In a tight labor market, one would think that employers would want any worker. But that was not the case with these employers.

In 1995, then-Governor Hunt instituted the Work First Program, which was designed to help families stay off welfare or move off welfare and into employment. Work First offered wage and other incentives to North Carolina employers for hiring these individuals. Work First clients may be disadvantaged by the extensive use of Hispanic social networks as a hiring tool. Further, once these workers do get an entry-level job, the fact that employers may be unwilling to accommodate their particular special needs puts them at a further disadvantage.

President Clinton signed the Personal Responsibility and Work Reform Act of 1996 (PRWORA) which mandates that 50% of those who were receiving welfare benefits be working by the year 2002. If the attitudes expressed in this study are widespread, this has serious implications for those workers required to get off welfare. If they are systematically excluded from informal job information networks in the entry-level labor market, this has implications for the success of programs like Work First, PRWORA, and for other recent federal programs such as the Workforce Investment Act of 1998 (WIA).

The general disenchantment most of these employers expressed toward native-born workers, both White and Black, together with the extremely favorable perception they held of Hispanic workers has implications for the success of programs like Work First. Incentives provided by the program may not be enough to make employers consider hiring these workers in light of the fact that they perceive Hispanics to have a superior work ethic and to contribute more to a harmonious work environment. Coupled with the impression that undocumented Hispanic workers may be more a more vulnerable and thus more pliable workforce in the eyes of North Carolina employers, this may make immigrants even harder for Work First participants to compete with in terms of entry level jobs.

Employer demand for labor has been shown in this study to be a very powerful impetus for Hispanic immigrants to come to North Carolina. The effective of U.S. immigration policy is brought into question by these results. Because employers were not particularly diligent in checking their Hispanic workers' documents and because they encouraged their Hispanic employees to refer their friends and family members, and in light of the fact that these North Carolina employers were ready to accept these workers and indeed encourage their presence in the labor market, efforts to stop immigrants at the border will fail. Employer demand must be addressed as a major factor in labor migration before any future policies designed to stem the tide of undocumented immigration are developed. Employer demand, the availability of jobs and the lure of higher wages are a very powerful force and the Immigration and Naturalization Service will not be able to stop these labor flows at the border.

Another important policy implication is the effect of the H-2A program on the influx of Hispanics to North Carolina. These employers felt that this program was a precursor to the influx and that many Hispanics who are now working in urban areas originally entered the country through this program. If a significant number of Hispanic workers in North Carolina urban areas entered the U.S. on an H-2A visa, this is a vivid example of an unintended effect of immigration policy.

Finally, this study was conducted during an economic boom in North Carolina. History is full of accounts of backlash against immigrants during economic downturns. Since shortly before the events of September 11, 2001, the U.S. economy has experienced an economic downturn. The results of this analysis have implications in this regard as well. Already anecdotal evidence exists of backlash being leveled against North Carolina immigrant Hispanics. In light of the attitudes expressed by some North Carolinians in the Carolina Poll data, as well as those in more recent public opinion research, tensions surrounding the labor force and the availability of jobs and other scarce resources could be further exacerbated by a sustained economic decline.

Since the passing of the Uniting and Strengthening America by Providing Appropriate Tools Required to Increase and Obstruct Terrorism Act of 2001 (USAPATRIOT), which widened the surveillance and investigative powers of law enforcement agencies, the vulnerability of undocumented workers has increased. Employers might also utilize the increased vulnerabilities of their Hispanic workers during an economic downturn to exploit them. Undocumented Hispanic workers might be in even greater demand during downturns precisely because they are vulnerable, and thus perceived by some employers to be less likely to complain about wages, benefits and working conditions.

Future Research

Future research should include interviews with immigrant Hispanic workers. Their impressions and motivations regarding the labor market and about their U.S. employers are important considerations and should be studied. Abuses of undocumented worker in North Carolina urban areas should be studied, particularly from the perspectives of these workers. The institution of the USAPATRIOT Act has made this an even more important issue for these workers. The prevalence of rural to urban movement (and from H-2A to undocumented status) should be studied further. The importance Hispanic workers place on employer demand as a pull factor should also be considered. Push factors are an important element that was not considered here. Any effective immigration policy must address the factors in Mexico and the rest of Latin America that contribute to the exodus of workers from those countries.

A more in-depth newspaper content analysis should be conducted, including analysis of Spanish-language newspapers. Whether the Spanish-language media in immigrant gateway communities were an important avenue of recruitment for North Carolina employers could then be documented. Locally, advertising on Spanish-language radio stations is probably a method of Hispanic labor recruitment that is growing in importance and should be studied. Future research should include interviews with coyotes and those who participate in the black market for documentation. Research of this aspect of the subject might give a vivid picture of Hispanic labor recruitment from abroad.

Two additional issues were touched on in the study and warrant further investigation. First, respondents generally agreed that most of the applicants with whom they interfaced were male. The 2000 Census figures supported this perception. The exceptions to this were the employers or intermediaries who had hired bi-lingual staff. These respondents reported a more balanced gender distribution. Perhaps female immigrant Hispanic workers are more comfortable applying at places of employment where they know the interviewers will speak their language.

The second issue was that of employer networks. Some of the employers in this study reported sharing information about Hispanic workers with each other. This assisted them in finding workers for themselves, for those they did business with, and for other people not directly related to their business but who recognized them as an establishment that had a number of Hispanic workers. This is a fascinating issue, in light of the tightness of the labor market. Evidence presented here overwhelmingly showed that employers often felt pitted against each other for labor. Studying the extent of the use of employer networks would be an interesting and relevant topic, and would reveal if this practice is prevalent in the Triangle and elsewhere.

Hispanic immigration has changed North Carolina communities in a myriad of ways. The Census 2000 confirms that immigration of Hispanic to North Carolina is not likely to end soon. The effects of this are far-reaching for communities in the state and North Carolina is being transformed into a multi-cultural and multi-race state in the new millennium.

APPENDICES

A. North Carolina Counties

B. Photocopies of Original Help Wanted Advertisements

Houston Chronicle, June 16, 1988

> ALBANILES Especializados. En Teja, No Se Necesita Experiencia. Prueba De Permiso De Tradajo Y Numero De Seguro Social. Llamar 305-488-1671. Despues de las 5. Por hora $6.50

Houston Chronicle, Nov. 16, 1988

> CAR WASH HELP Wanted in Charlotte NC, Louisville KY, Cincinnati OH. We are looking for hard workers who see themselves as winners. Top performance can earn up to $15,000/year. Se Habla Espanol. Interviews will be held in Houston on Nov. 8 & 9. Call Tom Krell at 704-537-3700 to arrange for interview

El Paso Times, June 1, 1980

> TILESETTERS Needed. Must know mud work. Residential & commercial jobs. Must be able to relocate to Riley, N. Carolina. Call collect 919-850-0010 or after 5. 919-859-5820.

Dallas Morning News, Nov. 26, 1988

> FAMILY to help on dairy farm (Mexican preferred). Must run machinery. Call 919-366-4806 after 8:00 p.m.

NOTES

[1] "Hispanic" is a label that has primarily come into use since the U.S. Census Bureau began to use it in 1980. The term "Hispanic" is used here as a broad category to mean those of Latin American ethnicity or descent. While acknowledging that many prefer the term "Latino," the author has chosen to use the label "Hispanic" precisely because Census data was used in the study, and because the Census Bureau defines the term clearly. On the same token, the term "Black" is used here in place of the term "African American" because the Census Bureau defines the term "Black" clearly as a race variable without regard to nationality or ethnicity.

[2] Family members were excluded from the quotas imposed by the IRCA legislation.

[3] See (Browning and M. 1979) for a discussion of the geographical boundaries of the Sunbelt.

[4] The Northeast includes Connecticut, Maine, Massachusetts, New Hampshire, New Jersey, New York, Pennsylvania, Rhode Island, and Vermont. The Midwest includes Illinois, Indiana, Iowa, Kansas, Michigan, Minnesota, Missouri, Nebraska, North Dakota, Ohio, South Dakota, and Wisconsin. The South includes Alabama, Arkansas, Delaware, the District of Columbia, Florida, Georgia, Kentucky, Louisiana, Maryland, Mississippi, North Carolina, Oklahoma, South Carolina, Tennessee, Texas, Virginia, and West Virginia. The West includes Alaska, Arizona, California, Colorado, Hawaii, Idaho, Montana, Nevada, New Mexico, Oregon, Utah, Washington, and Wyoming.

[5] The East South Central Division includes: Alabama, Mississippi, Tennessee and Kentucky. The West South Central Division includes Louisiana, Arkansas Oklahoma and Texas.

[6] Many of the high rates of growth experienced by these states are due to a relatively low baseline population of Hispanic population in 1990. This would not hold true, however, for states such as Illinois and Florida.

[7] The southern states are as follows: North Carolina (393.9%); Arkansas (337.0%); Georgia (299.6%); South Carolina (211.2%); Alabama (207.9%); Kentucky (172.9%); Mississippi (148.4%); Delaware (135.6%); Virginia (105.6%); Maryland (82.2%); and Florida (70.4%). The Midwestern states include: Minnesota (166.1%); Nebraska

(155.4%); Iowa (152.6%); Indiana (117.2%); South Dakota (107.6%); Wisconsin (107.0%); Kansas (101.0%); Missouri (92.2%); and Illinois (69.2%).

[8] The data are collected from respondents' answer to this question in the census: Residence in 1985?

[9] The Supplementary Survey data are based on a significantly smaller sample than are the PUMS (long form data). Therefore their accuracy, especially in connection with groups who have been historically underrepresented in the census counts, can be called into question. These data can, however, provide an interesting illustration of the migration patterns of Hispanics. Further, because the Census typically undercounts Hispanics, this means that these results may be understated. These data are the response to the question: Residence in 1999.

[10] Personal communication, M.E. Davis, Demographic Surveys Division, Continuous Measurement Office, U.S. Census Bureau, December 10, 2002.

[11] Chatham County is part of the Raleigh-Durham-Chapel Hill MSA.

[12] Following Roseman, 1977, an in-migration field is one in which 100 migrants move into an area.

[13] This passage was first published in (Johnson-Webb 2002), p. 413.

14 This passage was first published in (Johnson-Webb 2002), p.10.

[15] This passage was first published in (Johnson-Webb 2002), p. 8.

[16] This passage was first published in Johnson-Webb, 2002, p. 416.

[17] This figure has been transcribed from the originals advertisements. See Appendix B for photocopies of the originals, which were first published in Johnson-Webb, 2002, p. 414.

[18] This passage was first published in Johnson-Webb, 2002, p. 414.

[19] This passage was first published in (Johnson-Webb 2002), p.12.

[20] This passage was first published in (Johnson-Webb 2002), p. 415.

[21] This passage was first published in (Johnson-Webb 2002), p.12.

[22] This passage was first published in (Johnson-Webb 2002), p.11.

[23] This passage was first published in Johnson-Webb, 2002, p. 415.

WORKS CITED

Abbott, C. (1990). New West, New South, New Region: The Discovery of the Sunbelt. *Searching for the Sunbelt: Historical Perspectives on a Region.* R. A. Mohl. Knoxville, University of Tennessee Press.

Alba, R. D., J. R. Logan, et al. (2000). "The changing neighborhood contexts of the immigrant metropolis." *Social Forces 79*(2): 587-621.

Andrews, W. H. and S. Z. Nagi (1956). Migrant Agricultural Labor in Ohio. Wooster, OH, Ohio Agricultural Experimental Station.

Arango, J. (2000). "Global Trends and Issues: Explaining Migration: A Critical View." *International Social Science Journal 52*(165): 283-296.

ASN American Services Network, P. C. (1998). H-2A Visa, H-2B Visa. 1999.

Assiss, C. (2002). Organizado una Cena Mexicana. *Herald-Sun.* Durham, NC: C4.

Ayudate (2002). Latin Organizations-Organizaciones Latinas. 2002.

Baker, S. G. (1997). "The 'Amnesty' Aftermath: Current Policy Issues Stemming from the Legalization Programs of the 1986 Immigration Reform and Control Act." *International Migration Review 31*(1): 5-27.

Barkan, E. (1990). New Origins, New Homeland, New Region: American Immigration and the Emergence of the Sunbelt, 1955-1985. *Searching for the Sunbelt: Historical Perspectives on a Region.* R. A. Mohl. Knoxville, University of Tennessee Press.

Work Cited

Bartley, N. V. (1995). The Sunbelt South. *A History of the South: The New South 1945-1980*. Baton Rouge, University of Louisiana Press: 417-454.

Bean, F. and M. Tienda (1987). *Hispanics in the United States*. New York, Russel Sage.

Bean, F. D., J. Van Hook, et al. (1999). Immigration, Spatial and Economic Change, and African American Employment. *Immigration and Opportunity: Race, Ethnicity, and Employment in the United States*. F. D. Bean and S. Bell-Rose. New York, NY, Russell Sage Foundation: 31-63.

Berry, B. B. L. (1993). "Transnational Urbanward Migration, 1830-1980." *Annals of the Association of American Geographers* 83(3): 389-406.

Berry, B. B. L. and D. C. Dahmann (1977). Population Redistribution in the United States. Washington, DC, National Academy of Sciences.

Bettez, S. (1992). Hispanics 'Settling Out' of the Migration in North Carolina. *School of Social Work*. Chapel Hill, University of North Carolina at Chapel Hill.

Bickley, R. (1999). Notion of Hispanic Bank Again Discussed. *Raleigh News & Observer*. Raleigh, NC: 1.

Biggars, J. C. (1979). "The Sunning of America: Migration to the Sunbelt." *Population Bulletin* 34(1): 3-43.

Bluestone, B. and B. Harrison (1982). *The Deindustrialization of America*. New York, Basic Books.

Booth, W. (1998). The American Dream in the 1990s: At the Bottom of the Economic Ladder, There is Room Aplenty for Immigrants. *Washington Post National Weekly Edition*. Washington, DC: 8-10.

Works Cited

Borjas, G. J. (1990). *Friends or Strangers: The Impact of Immigrants on the US Economy.* New York, Basic Books.

Boswell, T. (1984). "The Migration and Distribution of Cubans and Puerto Ricans Living in the United States." *Journal of Geography*: 65-72.

Boswell, T. D., J. Nogel, et al. (2001). *Facts About Immigration: Asking 'Six Big Questions' for Florida and Miami-Dade County.* Miami, FL, University of Florida.

Bouvier, L. F. and R. W. Gardner (1986). "Immigration the US: The Unfinished Story." *Population Bulletin 41*(4): 1-51.

Branson, R. (1997). Immigrants Changing Dixie. *Commercial Appeal.* Nashville, TN: 5.

Briggs, V., Jr. (1984). *Immigration Policy and the American Labor Force.* Baltimore, The Johns Hopkins Press.

Briggs, V., Jr. (1996). *Mass Immigration and the National Interest.* Armonk, NY, M.E. Sharpe.

Broadway, M. (1995). From City to Countryside: Recent Changes in the Structure and Locales of the Meat- and Fish-Processing Industries. *Any Way You Cut It: Meat Processing and Small-Town America.* D. Stull, M. Broadway and G. D. C. Lawrence, KS, University of Kansas Press.

Broadway, M. J. (2000). "Planning for Change in Small Towns or Trying to Avoid the Slaughterhouse Blues." *Journal of Rural Studies 16*: 27-46.

Browning, C. E. and G. W. M. (1979). "The Sun Belt-Snow Belt: A Case of Sloppy Regionalizing." *Professional Geographer 31*(1): 66-74.

Capelli, P. (1995). "Is the 'Skills Gap' Really About Attitudes?" *California Management Review 37*(4): 108-124.

Cardenas, G. (1978). "Los Desarraigados: Chicanos in the Midwestern United States." *Aztlan* 7(2): 153-186.

Carlson, A. W. (1975). "The Settling Process of Mexican-Americans in Northwest Ohio." *Journal of Mexican-American History* 5(1): 24-42.

Carter, M. (1999). Soccer League Scores big with area Hispanics. *Raleigh News & Observer*. Raleigh, NC: 5.

Carter, T. A. (2002). The North Carolina Poultry Industry. Raleigh, NC, North Carolina State University Extension Poultry Science: 1-10.

Cherry, A.-E. (1995). Organized and Planned Patterns of Movement of Migrant Farmworkers in Selected Counties in North Carolina. *Geography and Urban Planning*. Boone, NC, Appalachian State University.

Chio, W. A. (1971). The Migration of Mexican-American Agricultural Labor into Wood County, Ohio, 1970. *Geography*. Bowling Green, OH, Bowling Green State University.

Cobb, J. C. (1990). The Sunbelt South: Industrialization in Regional, National and International Perspective. *Searching for the Sunbelt: Historical Perspectives on a Region*. R. A. Mohl. Knoxville, University of Tennessee Press.

Cobb, J. C. (1993). *The Selling of the South: The Southern Crusade for Industrial Development, 1936-1990*. Chicago, University of Illinois Press.

Cohen, L. P. (1998). Meatpacker Taps Mexican Labor Force, Thanks to Help from an INS Program. *Wall Street Journal*. New York, NY: 1.

Conover, T. (1987). *Coyotes*. New York, Basic Books.

Cooper, M. (1997). The Heartland's Raw Deal: How Meatpacking is Creating a New Underclass. *The Nation*: 11-17.

Works Cited

Cooper, R. T. (2001). Racial Ethnic Diversity Puts New Face on Middle American; Census: The Upper Midwest, and Other Once-Homogeneous Areas, Find Challenging Changes. *Los Angeles Times*. Los Angeles, CA: 1.

Cornelius, W. A. (1998). The Structural Embeddedness of Demand for Mexican Immigrant Labor: New Evidence from California. *Crossings: Mexican Immigration in Interdisciplinary Perspectives*. M. M. Suárez-Orozco. Cambridge, MA, Harvard University David Rockefeller Center for Latin American Studies: 113-155.

County Commissioners (2000). News Release. Chapel Hill, NC, Orange County Board of County Commissioners.

Cravey, A. J. (1997). "Latino Labor and Poultry Production in Rural North Carolina." *Southeastern Geographer XXXVII*(2): 295-300.

Cromartie, J. and C. B. Stack (1989). "Reinterpretation of Black Return Migration to the South, 1975-1980." *Geographical Review 79*: 297-310.

Dagodag, T. (1984). Illegal Mexican Aliens in Los Angeles: Locational Characteristics. *Patterns of Undocumented Migration: Mexico and the US*. R. C. Jones. Totowa, NJ, Rowman and Allenheld.

Dagodag, T. (1984). Illegal Mexican Immigration to California from Western Mexico. *Patterns of Undocumented Migration: Mexico and the US*. R. C. Jones. Totowa, NJ, Rowman and Allenheld.

Daniels, M. (1997). "Warm Areas Continue Hottest Job Growth." *Monthly Labor Review 120*(7): 43-44.

Davis, T., P. Gildner, et al. (1997). Latino Community of Wake County: A Community Diagnosis Including Secondary Data Analysis and Qualitative Data Collection, University of North Carolina at Chapel Hill.

Decierdo, M. (1991). "A Mexican Migrant Family in North Carolina." *Aztlan* 20(1 & 2): 183-193.

DeJong, G. F. and Q.-G. Tran (2001). "Warm Welcome, Cool Welcome: Mapping Receptivity Toward Immigrants in the U.S." *Population Today* 29(8): 1, 4-5.

Delechat, C. (2001). "International Migration Dynamics: The Role of Experience and Social Networks." *Labour* 15(3): 457-486.

Desbarats, J. (1985). "Indochinese resettlement in the United States." *Annals of the Association of American Geographers* 75(4): 522-538.

Edson, G. T. (1927). Mexicans in Our Northcentral States. Berkeley, CA, Bancroft Library.

Effland, A. B. and K. Kassel (1996). Hispanics in Rural America: The Influence of Immigration and Language on Economic Well-Being. *Rural/Ethnic Minorities in Rural Areas : Progress and Stagnation, 1980-1990*. L. L. Swanson. Washington, EC, USDA. ERS: 87-99.

Eisley, M. (2000). Mexico to open office in NC. *Raleigh News & Observer*. Raleigh, NC: 1.

Employment Policy Foundation (2001). "Immigration is Critical To Future Growth and Competitiveness." *Policy Backgrounder* (June 11).

Espenshade, T. J. (1997). "Unauthorized Immigration to the United States." *Annual Reviews of Sociology* 21: 195-216.

Faught, J. D. (1976). "Chicanos in a Medium-Sized City: Demographic and Socioeconomic Characteristics." *Aztlan* 7(2): 307-329.

Fimmen, C., D. Riggins, et al. (1997). Connecting the Parts: A Hispanic/Latino Reality for Achieving More Timely Degree Completion, JSRI.

Fischer, C., Ed. (1998). *Gale Directory of Publications and Broadcast Media.* Detroit, MI, Gale Research.

Foust, D. and M. Mallory (1993). The Boom Belt: There's No Speed Limit on Growth Along the South's I-85. *Business Week*: 98-104.

Frey, W. H. (1993). "The New Urban Revival in the United States." *Urban Studies 30*: 741-775.

Frey, W. H. (1995). "Immigration and Internal Migration: Flight from US Metropolitan Areas: Toward a New Demographic Balkanization." *Urban Studies 64*(4-5): 733-757.

Frey, W. H. and K.-L. Liaw (1998). "Immigrant Concentration and Domestic Dispersal: Is Movement to Nonmetropolitan Areas 'White Flight'?" *Professional Geographer 50*(2): 215-232.

Frey, W. H., K.-L. Liaw, et al. (1995). Interstate Migration of the US Poverty Population: Immigration 'Pushes' and Welfare Magnet 'Pull'. Ann Arbor, Population Studies Center of the University of Michigan.

Furtaw, J., Ed. (1992). *Hispanic Americans Information Directory, 1992-1993.* Detroit, MI, Gale Research.

Gamio, M. (1930). *Mexican Immigration to the United States.* Chicago, Univ of Chicago Press.

Garcia, J. R. (1979). The People of Mexican Descent in Michigan: A Historical Overview. *Blacks and Chicanos in Urban Michigan.* H. C. Hawkins and R. W. Thomas. Lansing, Michigan History Division, Michigan Department of State: 44-56.

Garrett, A. (1997). Police anticipate arrests in crimes targeting Hispanics. *Raleigh News & Observer.* Raleigh, NC: 3.

Gilbert, E. (1996). Changing Demographics Have Created New Market Opportunities and Prompted St. Paul Fire and Marine to Form a

Multicultural Business Group. *Underwriter Property and Casualty*: 33.

Glascock, N. (1999). INS' quick response team' arrives in Triangle. *Raleigh News & Observer*. Raleigh, NC: 1.

Glascock, N. (2000). Town prepares for worst from hate group. *Raleigh News & Observer*. Raleigh, NC: 1.

Glick, J. E. and J. Van Hook (2001). "Parents' Coresidence with Adult Children: Can Immigration Explain Race and Ethnic Variation?" *Journal of Marriage and the Family* (forthcoming).

Gober, P. (1993). "Americans on the Move." *Population Bulletin 48*(3): 1-39.

Goss, J. and B. Lindquist (1995). "Conceptualizing International Migration: A Structural Perspective." *International Migration Review 29*(2): 317-351.

Gouveia, L. and R. Saenz (2000). "Global Forces and Latino Population Growth in the Midwest: A Regional and Subregional Analysis." *Great Plains Research 10*(Fall): 305-328.

Gouveia, L. and D. Stull (1995). Dances with Cows: Beefpacking's Impact on Garden City, KS and Lexington, NE. *Any Way You Cut It: Meat Processing and Small-Town America*. D. Stull, M. Broadway and D. C. Griffith. Lawrence, KS, University of Kansas Press.

Green, S. (1994). Del Valle a Willmar: Settling Out of the Migrant Stream in a Rural Minnesota Community. East Lansing, MI, Julian Samora Research Institute, Michigan State University,.

Grey, M. (1995). Pork, Poultry and Newcomers in Storm Lake, Iowa. *Any Way You Cut It: Meat Processing and Small-Town America*. D. Stull, M. Broadway and D. C. Griffith. Lawrence, KS, University of Kansas Press.

Griffith, D. C. (1990). "Consequences of Immigration Reform for Low-Wage Workers in the Southeaster U.S. : The Case of the Poultry Industry." *Urban Anthropology* 19(1-2): 155-184.

Griffith, D. C. (1993). *Jones's Minimal: Low-wage Labor in the United States*. Albany, State University of New York Press.

Griffith, D. C. (1995). Hay Trabajo. *Any Way You Cut It: Meat Processing and Small-Town America*. D. Stull, M. Broadway and D. C. Griffith. Lawrence, KS, University of Kansas Press.

Griffith, D. C. and D. Runsten (1992). "The Impact of the 1986 Immigration Reform and Control Act on the US Poultry Industry: A Comparative Analysis." *Policy Studies Review* 11(2): 118-130.

Grosfoguel, R. and H. CorderoGuzman (1998). "International Migration in a Global Context: Recent Approaches to Migration Theory." *Diaspora* 7(3): 351-368.

Guzman, B. (2001). The Hispanic Population. Washington, DC, U.S. Census Bureau.

Haney, J. B. (1979). Chicanos of Michigan. *Blacks and Chicanos in Urban Michigan*. H. C. Hawkins and R. W. Thomas. Lansing, Michigan History Division, Michigan Department of State: 17-19.

Hart, J. F. and C. Mayda (1998). "The Industrialization of Livestock Production in the United States." *Southeastern Geographer* 38(1): 58-78.

Harvey, D. (1989). *The Condition of Postmodernity: An Enquiry into the Origins of Cultural Change*. Oxford [England], Cambridge, MA, Blackwell.

Heckman, J. J. (2000). "Understanding Black-White Wage Differentials, 1960-1990." *American Economic Review* 90(2): 344-49.

Hedges, S. J., D. Hawkins, et al. (1996). The New Jungle. *US News & World Report*: 34-45.

Hendee, D. (1997). Population Changes Worry Rural Residents: The Latest Rural Nebraska Poll Gauges Attitudes about Communities. *Omaha World Herald*. Omaha, NE: 1.

Hirschman, C., P. Kasinitz, et al., Eds. (1999). *The Handbook of International Migration: The American Experience*. New York, Russell Sage Foundation.

Holzer, H. J. (1987). Hiring Procedures in the Firm: Their Economic Determinants and Outcomes. *Human Resources and the Performance of the Firm, 1987*. S. G. Allen and M. M. Kleiner. Madison, WI, Industrial Relations Research Association.

Holzer, H. J. (1996). *What Employers Want: Job Prospects for Less-Educated Workers*. New York, Russell Sage.

Howlett, D. (1995). Midwest New Hub for Hispanics. *USA Today*: 3.

Hughes, C. (2000). Latino Population Soars along with Opportunities. *Blade*. Toledo, OH: A1.

Hull, A. (2001). In N.C., Anxiety and Animosity Put an Edge on an Old Dream. *Washington Post*. Washington, DC: A1, A18.

Hull, A. (2002). Old South Goes With the Wind: Entrepreneur and His Workers Reflect Region's Racial Transformation. *Washington Post*. Washington, DC: A01.

Humphrey, N. D. (1943). "The Migration and Settlement of Detroit Mexicans." *Economic Geography* 19(4): 358-361.

Humphreys, D. (1993). "Hispanic Buying Power by Place of Residence." *Georgia Business and Economic Conditions* 58(6): 1-8.

Iredale, R. (2001). "The Migration of Professionals: Theories and Typologies." *International Migration* 39(5): 7-26.

Works Cited

Johnson, J. H. (1998). The Two Faces of North Carolina: An Action Agenda," Keynote Address. North Carolina Association of Community Foundations. Chapel Hill, North Carolina.

Johnson, J. H. and W. C. Farrell (1993). "The Fire This Time: The Genesis of the Los Angeles Rebellion of 1992." *North Carolina Law Review* 71(5): 1043-1020.

Johnson, J. H., W. C. Farrell, et al. (1997). "Immigration Reform and the Browning of America: Tensions, Conflict, and Community Instability." *International Migration Review* 31(4): 1055-1095.

Johnson, J. H. and D. M. Grant (1997). "Post-1980 Black Population Redistribution Trends in the US." *Southeastern Geographer* 37(1): 1-19.

Johnson, J. H., K. D. Johnson-Webb, et al. (1999). Newly Emerging Hispanic Communities in the US: A Spatial Analysis of Settlement Patterns, In-Migration Fields, and Social Receptivity. *Immigration and Opportunity: Race, Ethnicity and Employment in the United States*. F. Bean and S. Bell-Rose. New York, Russell Sage.

Johnson, J. H., K. D. Johnson-Webb, et al. (1999). "Profile of North Carolina Hispanics." *Popular Government*(Fall): 2-12.

Johnson, J. H. and M. Oliver (1989). "Interethnic Conflict in Urban America: The Effects of Economic and Social Dislocations." *Urban Geography* 10: 449-463.

Johnson, J. H. and C. C. Roseman (1990). "Increasing Black Out-migration from Los Angeles: The Role of Household Dynamics and Kinship Systems." *Annals of the Association of American Geographers* 80(2): 205-222.

Johnson-Webb, K. D. (1999). "Hispanics are Changing the Face of North Carolina." *Common Sense*(Spring): 8-16.

Johnson-Webb, K. D. (2001). "Midwest Rural Communities in Transition: Hispanic Immigrants." *Rural Development News* 25(1): 4-5.

Johnson-Webb, K. D. (2002). ""Workfare" in the Triangle: Local Context and Employer Biases Against Welfare Recipients." *Southeastern Geographer* 42(1): 1-19.

Johnson-Webb, K. D. and J. H. Johnson (1996). "North Carolina Communities in Transition: The Hispanic Influx." *North Carolina Geographer* 5(Winter): 21-40.

Jones, R. C. (1982). "Channelization of Undocumented Mexican Migrants to the US." *Economic Geography* 58(2): 156-176.

Jones, R. C. (1984). Macro-Patterns of Undocumented Migration Between Mexico and the US, in Patterns of Undocumented Migration: Mexico and the US. *Patterns of Undocumented Migration: Mexico and the US*. R. C. Jones. Totowa, N.J., Rowman and Allanheld.

Kane, D. (1988). La Casa Multicultural helping Hispanics fight crime. *Raleigh News & Observer*. Raleigh, N.C.: 1.

Kirschenman, J. and K. Neckerman (1990). We'd Love to Hire Them But... *The Urban Underclass*. C. Jencks and P. Petersen. Washington, D.C, Brookings Institution.

Krouse, P. (1997). Land of Opportunity: Hispanics immigrants find plenty of job openings in a business climate eager for new workers. *Greensboro News & Record*. Greensboro, N.C.: 1.

Labich, K. (1994). The Geography of an Emerging America. *Fortune*. *129*: 88-93.

Lee, E. (1966). "A Theory of Migration." *Demography* 3(1): 47-57.

Lee, S. W. and C. C. Roseman (1997). "Independent and Linked Migrants: Determinant of African American Interstate Migration." *Growth and Change* 50(2): 204-215.

Works Cited

Levin, K., L. Rolon, et al. (1995). Latinos in Siler City: Community Perspectives. Chapel Hill, NC, School of Public Health

University of North Carolina at Chapel Hill.

Levin, K., K. Schlanger, et al. (1995). A Community Diagnosis of the Latino Community in Siler City. Chapel Hill, NC, School of Public Health

University of North Carolina at Chapel Hill.

Li, W. (1998). "Los Angeles's Chinese ethnoburb: From ethnic service center to global economy outpost." *Urban Geography* 19(6): 502-517.

Lieberson, S. and M. Waters (1987). "The Location of Ethnic and Racial Groups in the United States." *Sociological Forum* 2(4): 780-810.

Long, L. (1988). *Migration and Residential Mobility in the United Stat.* New York, NY, Russel Sage.

Long, L. and K. Hansen (1975). "Trends in Return Migration to the South." *Demography* 12(4): 601-614.

Longino, C. F. (1994). "From Sunbelt to Sunspot." *American Demographics* 16(11): 22-30.

Macklin, J. (1958). Preliminary Report on Americans of Mexican Descent. Toledo, OH, Board of Community Relations.

Massey, D., J. Arango, et al. (1993). "Theories of International Migration: A Review and Appraisal." *Population and Development Review* 19(3): 431-466.

Massey, D., J. Arango, et al. (1994). "An Evaluation of International Migration Theory: The North American Case." *Population and Development Review* 20(4): 699-751.

Massey, D. S. (1999). Why Does Immigration Occur? A Theoretical Synthesis. *The International Handbook of International Migration: The American Experience*. C. Hirschman, P. Kasinitz and J. DeWind. New York, Russell Sage Foundation.

McDowell, L. (1997). Appendix: Field Work. *Capital Culture: Gender at Work in the City*. Oxford, Blackwell Publishers.

McHugh, K. (1987). "Black Migration Reversal in the United States." *Geographical Review* 77(2): 171-182.

McHugh, K. (1989). "Hispanic Migration and Population Redistribution in the US." *Professional Geographer* 41(4): 429-439.

McHugh, K., I. Miyares, et al. (1997). "The Magnetism of Miami: Segmented paths in Cuban Migration." *Geographical Review* 87(4): 504-519.

McWilliams, C. (1948). *North from Mexico: The Spanish-Speaking People of the United States*. New York, NY, Greenwood Press.

MDC, I. (2002). State of the Region 2002: Shadows in the Sunbelt Revisited. Chapel Hill, NC, MDC, Inc.

Melcher, R. and K. Kelly (1994). America's Heartland: The Midwest's New Role in the Global Economy. *Business Week*: 116-124.

Mincy, R. B. (1993). The Urban Institute Audit Studies: Their Research and Policy Context. *Clear and Convincing Evidence: Measurement of Discrimination in America*. M. Fix and R. J. Struck. Washington, DC, Urban Institute Press.

Miyares, I. (1997). "Changing Perceptions of Space and Place as a Measure of Hmong Acculturation." *Professional Geographer* 49(2): 214-225.

Moss, P. and C. Tilly (1995). "Skills and Race in Hiring: Quantitative Findings from Face-to-Face Interviews." *Eastern Economic Journal* 21(3): 357-374.

Works Cited

Moss, P. and C. Tilly (1996). "'Soft Skills' and Race: An Investigation of Black Men's Employment Problems." *Work and Occupations* 23(3): 252-276.

Muller, T. (1984). The Fourth Wave: California's Newest Immigrants. Washington, DC, Urban Institute Press.

Nasser, H. E. (2001). Immigration Helped Restore Cities '21st Century Could See an Urban Boom'. *USA Today*. McLean, VA: 3.

NCASA (2002). North Carolina Amateur Soccer Association, NCASA. 2002.

Nelson, M. (1990). Migrant and Immigrants (Mexicans in North Carolina. *Southern Historical Collection*. Chapel Hill, NC, Wilson Library.

Newbold, K. B. (1999). "Internal migration of the foreign-born: Population concentration or dispersion?" *Population and Environment* 20(3): 259-276.

Newbold, K. B. (2000). "Separate destinations: Migration, immigration and the politics of places." *Growth and Change* 31(3): 441-443.

Newbold, K. B. and J. Spindler (2001). "Immigrant settlement patterns in metropolitan Chicago." *Urban Studies* 38(11): 1903-1919.

Oliver, M. and J. H. Johnson (1984). "Interethnic Conflict in an Urban Ghetto: The Case of Blacks and Latinos in Los Angeles." *Research in Social Movements* 6: 57-94.

Piore, M. (1979). *Birds of Passage*. Cambridge, Cambridge University Press.

Plane, D. A. and A. M. Isserman (1983). "US Interstate Labor Force Migration: An Analysis of Trends, Net Exchanges, and Migration Subsystems." *Socio-Economic Planning Science* 17(5-6): 251-266.

Pollard, K. M. and W. P. O'Hare (1999). "America's Racial and Ethnic Minorities." *Population Bulletin 54*(3): 3-48.

Portes, A. (1978). "Migration and Underdevelopment." *Politics & Society 8*(1): 1-48.

Portes, A. (1996). Immigration Theory for a New Century: Some Problems and Opportunities. Sanibel Island, FL, Becoming American/America Becoming, Social Science Research Council Conference.

Portes, A. and R. L. Bach (1985). *Latin Journey*. Berkeley, University of California Press.

Portes, A. and R. Rumbaut (1996). *Immigrant America: A Portrait*. Berkeley, CA, University of California Press.

Portes, A. and Sensenbrenner (1993). "Embeddedness and Immigration: Notes on the Social Determinants of Economic Action." *American Journal of Sociology 98*(6).

Raleigh News & Observer (1999). Ethnic Markets. *Raleigh News & Observer*. Raleigh, NC: 15.

Rathge, R. and P. Highman (1998). "Population Change in the Great Plains: A History of Prolonged Decline." *Rural Development Perspectives 13*(1): 19-25.

Ravenstein, E. G. (1885). "The Laws of Migration, Pt. I." *Journal of the Royal Statistical Society 48*.

Ravenstein, E. G. (1889). "The Laws of Migration, Pt. II." *Journal of the Royal Statistical Society 52*.

Reddy, S. (1999). Parents fear ethnic shift in Chatham. *Raleigh News & Observer*. Raleigh, NC: 1.

Ribadeneira, D. (1996). Hispanics Find Warm Welcome in Cold Midwest. *Boston Globe*. Boston, MA: 3.

Robles, a. (1997). Newspapers vie for growing Latino market. *Raleigh News & Observer*. Raleigh, NC: 1.

Rochin, R. (2000). "Latinos in the Great Plains: An Overview." *Great Plains Research 10*(Fall): 243-52.

Rood, L. (1999). Iowa's Immigrants Confidently Show Political Muscle," Des Moines Register. *Des Moines Register*. Des Moines, IA: 1.

Roseman, C. C. (1971). "Migration as a Spatial and Temporal Process." *Annals of the Association of American Geographers 61*(4): 589-598.

Roseman, C. C. (1977). Changing Migration Patterns within the United States. Washington, DC, Association of American Geographers.

Roseman, C. C. and S. W. Lee (1998). "The Changing Ethnic Map of the United States." *Professional Geographer 50*(2): 204-214.

Rosenbaum, R. P. (1993). "Farm Labor Organizing Committee: Grassroots Organizing for the Empowerment of the Migrant Farmworker Community." *Culture and Agriculture*(47): 21-23.

Ross, K., D. Hart, et al. (2002). Economic System Rests on Fragile House of Cards. *Chapel Hill News*. Chapel Hill, NC: 1.

Saenz, R. (1991). "Interregional Migration Patterns of Chicanos: The Core, Periphery, and Frontier." *Social Science Quarterly 72*(1): 37-52.

Saenz, R. and C. M. Cready (1997). The Southwest-Midwest Mexican American Migration Flows, 1985 -1990, JSRI.

Salt, J. (1989). "A Comparative Overview of International Trends and Types, 1950-1980." *International Migration Review 23*(3): 431-456.

Sanchez, M. (2001). Programs to Aid Hispanics Reach for Suburbs and Beyond. *Kansas City Star*. Kansas City, KS: B2.

Saporito, B. (1994). The World's Best Cities for Business. *Fortune Magazine*: 112-142.

Sassen, S. (1991). *The Global City*. New York, NY, Princeton University Press.

Sassen, S. (1996). "New Employment Regimes in Cities: The Impact on Immigrant Workers." *new community* 22(4): 579-594.

Sassen-Koob, S. (1981). "Towards a Conception of Immigrant Labor." *Social Problems* 29(1): 65-85.

Schoenberger, E. (1989). "Some Dilemmas of Automation: Strategic and Operational Aspects of Technological Change in Production." *Economic Geography* 65: 232-247.

Schoenberger, E. (1990). "US Manufacturing Investments in Western Europe: Markets, Corporate Strategy and Competitive Environment." *Annals of the Association of American Geographers* 80(3): 379-393.

Schoenberger, E. (1991). "The Corporate Interview as a Research Method in Economic Geography." *Professional Geographer* 43(2): 180-189.

Schorr, A. E. (1992). *Hispanic Resource Directory, 1992-1994*. Juneau, AK, Denali Press.

Schulman, D. (2000). Symposium to evaluate county soccer needs, recommend action. *Raleigh News & Observer*. Raleigh, NC: 3.

Sheehan, R. (1999). DMV out to 'get it right' for Hispanic customers. *Raleigh News & Observer*. Raleigh, NC: 1.

Simon, S. (1999). In Insular Iowa, a Jolt of Worldliness. *Los Angeles Times*. Los Angeles.

Sinclair, U. (1906). *The Jungle*. New York, NY, Doubleday.

Smith, J. P. and B. Edmonston, Eds. (1997). *The New Americans: Economic, Demographic, and Fiscal Effects of Immigration.* Washington, DC, National Academy Press.

Stawowy, M. (1998). Creation of Hispanic Council Historic Event. *Durham Herald Sun.* Durham, NC: 1.

Stevens, T. (1999). Winning influence. *Raleigh News & Observer.* Raleigh, NC: 5.

Stocking, B. (1997). Quietly, blacks and Latinos seek common ground. *Raleigh News & Observer.* Raleigh, NC: 20.

Stocking, B. (1997). Side by Side: Worlds apart, Pt 1. *Raleigh News & Observer.* Raleigh, NC: 1.

Stocking, B. (1998). Latinos on the Move to a New Promised Land. *San Jose Mercury News.* San Jose, CA: 1.

Stocking, B. (1998). Middle America Grapples with an Influx of Latinos. *San Jose Mercury News.* San Jose, CA: 12.

Stull, D., M. Broadway, et al., Eds. (1995). *Any Way You Cut It: Meat Processing and Small-Town America.* Lawrence, KS, University of Kansas Press.

Sugrue, T. J. (1993). The Structures of Urban Poverty: The Reorganization of Space and Work in Three Periods of American History. *The "Underclass" Debate.* M. B. Katz. Princeton, NJ, Princeton University Press.

Suro, R. and A. Singer (2002). Latino Growth in Metropolitan America: Changing Patterns, New Locations. Washington DC, Brookings Institution Center on Urban & Metropolitan Policy and The Pew Hispanic Trust.

Thompson, S. (2001). A Troubled Journey. *Chapel Hill News*. Chapel Hill, NC: 1.

Tienda, M. (1983). Residential Distribution and Internal Migration Patterns of Chicanos: A Critical Assessment. *The State of Chicano Research in Family, Labor and Migration Studies*. A. Valdez, A. Camarillo and T. Almaguer. Stanford, CA, Stanford Center for Chicano Research.

Tyner, J. A. (1996). "The Gendering of Philippine International Labor Migration." *Professional Geographer 48*(4): 403-416.

U.S. Bureau of Census (1993). Census of Population and Housing, 1990: Public Use Microdata Samples: Technical Documentation, Government Printing Office. 1997.

U.S. Census Bureau (2000). 2000 Census of Population and Housing. Washington, DC, Department of Commerce.

Valdez, A. and R. C. Jones (1984). Geographical Patterns of Undocumented Mexicans and Chicanos in San Antonio, Texas: 1970 and 1980. *Patterns of Undocumented Migration: Mexico and the US*. R. C. Jones. Totowa, NJ, Rowman and Allanheld.

Van Hook, J., J. E. Glick, et al. (1999). "Immigrant and Native Public Assistance Receipt: How the Unit of Analysis Affects Research Findings." *Demography 36*(1): 111-120.

Vargas, Z. (1999). *Proletarians of the North: A History of Mexican Industrial Workers in Detroit and the Midwest, 1917-1933*. Berkeley, CA, University of California Press.

von Sternberg, B. (2001). Beyond the Census; Twin Cities Have Become Magnet for State's Population. *Minneapolis Tribune*. Minneapolis, MN: A1.

Wagner, J. (1999). Hispanic named to Board of Education. Raleigh News & Observer. Raleigh, NC: 3.

Waldinger, R. (1989). "Immigration and Urban Change." *Annual Review of Sociology* 15: 211-232.

Waldinger, R. (1993). Who makes the Beds... Who Washes the Dishes?: Black/ Immigrant Competition Reassessed. Los Angeles, Institute of Industrial Relations, University of California-Los Angeles.

Waldinger, R. (1997). "Black/Immigrant Competition Re-Assessed: New Evidence from Los Angeles." *Sociological Perspectives* 40(3): 365-387.

Waldrauch, H. (1995). "Theories on Migration and Migration Policy (Theorien zu Migration und Migrationspolitik)." *Journal fur Sozialforschung* 35(1): 27-49.

Waldrop, K. B. (2001). Poultry Industry Holds Top Spot in Mississippi. *Agricultural News*, Mississippi State University Office of Agricultural Communications.

Walker, R., M. Ellis, et al. (1992). "Linked Migration Systems: Immigration and Internal Labor Flows in the United States." *Economic Geography* 68(3): 234-248.

Walker, R. and W. Hannan (1989). "Dynamic Settlement Processes: The Case of US Immigration." *Professional Geographer* 41(2): 172-183.

Weeks, J. R. and J. S. Benitez (1979). The Cultural Demography of Midwestern of Midwestern Chicano Communities. *The Chicano Experience*. S. West. Boulder, CO, Westview Press.

Wilson, T. D. (1993). "Theoretical Approaches to Mexican Wage Labor Migration." *Latin American Perspectives* 20(3): 98-129.

Wilson, W. J. (1987). *The Truly Disadvantaged*. Chicago, IL, University of Chicago Press.

Wilson, W. J. (1996). The Meaning and Significance of Race: Employers and Inner City Workers. *When Work Disappears: The World of the New Urban Poor.* New York, NY, Alfred A. Knopf.

Wolpert, J. (1965). "Behavioral Aspects of the Decision to Migrate." *Papers and Proceedings of the Regional Science Association* *15*: 159-169.

Zelinsky, W. (1971). "The Hypothesis of the Mobility Transition." *Geographical Review 61*(2): 210-249.

Zelinsky, W. and B. Lee (1998). "Heterolocalism: An Alternative Model of Sociospatial Behavior of Immigrant Ethnic Communities." *International Journal of Population Geography 4*: 281-298.

Zolberg, A. (1989). "The Next Waves: Migration Theory for a Changing World." *International Migration Review 22*(3): 403-429.

Zolberg, A. (1990). Reforming the Back Door: The Immigration Reform and Control Act of 1986 in Historical Perspective. *Immigration Reconsidered: History, Sociology, and Politics.* Yans-McLaughlin. New York, NY, Oxford University Press.

Zolberg, A. R. (1995). From Invitation to Interdiction: U.S. Foreign Policy and Immigration Since 1945. *Threatened Peoples, Threatened Borders: World Migration & U.S. Policy.* T. M. S. and M. Welner. New York, NY, W.W. Norton.

INDEX

Census Data
  Census 2000, 32, 35, 36, 37, 38, 40, 43, 44, 45, 50, 51, 120
  Census of Housing and Population, 1990, 35, 36, 37, 40, 43, 44, 50
  PUMS, Public Use Microdata Samples, 1990, 5, 6, 38, 52, 53, 54, 70, 124

Community Relations
  Blacks and Hispanics, 66
  Carolina Poll, 63, 64, 65, 118
  Hispanic organizations, 59, 60
  tensions and conflicts, 42, 46, 62
  use of public facilities, 61

Definition of Terms, 4

Demographic Change
  gender, 76, 119
  Hispanic births, 57
  rural, 46
  South Census Region, 36
  U.S., 31

Economic Restructuring, 7, 16, 17, 21, 29, 97

Education
  Hispanic school enrollments, 62

Employers
  accommodations, *see* Recruitment strategies, 102, 103, 115, 116
  attitudes, 24
  preferences
    work ethic, 25, 28, 79, 82, 83, 84, 97, 99, 104, 106, 113, 114, 115, 117
  recruitment strategies, 26, 72, 102, 113, 114, 116

Employment
  ESC, NC Employment Security Commission, 72, 73, 74, 92, 93, 96, 115
  hospitality industry, 75, 110, 113, 116
  meat-packing, 18, 19, 39
  migrant agricultural workers, 48, 93
  occupational typology, 72
  poultry-processing, 14, 18, 19, 20, 24, 25, 27, 41, 58, 75, 109, 110
  undocumented workers, 13, 14, 26, 62, 66, 79, 106, 107, 108, 115, 117, 118, 119

Employment Intermediaries
  coyotes, 26, 119
  temporary agencies, 26, 74, 91, 97, 102, 115

Geographic scale, 12, 16, 21, 22, 42, 45, 71

Hispanic
  buying power, 41
  ethnicity
    Cuban, 5, 23, 32, 48, 51, 94
    Mexican, 31, 50

Puerto Rican, 5, 31, 32, 50, 51, 93
labor recruitment, *see* Recruitment strategies, 76, 84, 97, 119
Hispanics
  demographics
    age distibution, 51
    gender, 76, 119
  history in the Midwest, 39
  school enrollments, 62
  soccer leagues, 60, 61
Immigrants
  immigration gateways, 20, 21, 32, 38, 46, 53, 62
  refugees, 23, 32
  undocumented, 13, 14, 26, 62, 66, 79, 106, 107, 108, 115, 117, 118, 119
INS, Immigration and Naturalization Service, 6, 61, 107
Mexico
  Consulates, 61, 95
  Mexican Consulate in Raleigh, 61
Migration
  counterurbanization, 22
  internal
    in-migration fields, 70
    return migration to the South, 21
  see Migration Theory, 12, 28
Migration Research
  geographic research, 75
Migration Theory
  dual labor market, 28, 116
  gaps in, 27, 28
  global cities, 11, 16, 17, 27, 69
  neo-classical, 27
  Ravenstein, 10
  social networks, 12, 17, 25, 28, 116, 117
  transnational migration, 9, 20
  world systems theory, 11, 28, 69
Migration Theory:, 10, 11, 27
Migration:, 21
North Carolina
  Chapel Hill, 20, 23, 48, 56, 61, 64, 65, 70, 71, 92
  Chatham County, 20, 62, 101, 103, 110, 124
  Siler City, 20, 62, 66
  Durham, 20, 23, 48, 60, 66, 69, 70, 110
  Employment Security Commission, 72, 73, 74, 92, 93, 96, 115
  Hispanic births, 57
  Hispanic Ombudsman, 61
  Hispanic organizations, 59, 60
    El Centro Hispano, 66
    El Pueblo, Inc., 56
  Hispanic owned businesses, *see tiendas*, 58
  Hispanics
    age distribution, 51
    ethnicity, 51
    gender, 76, 119
  I-85 corridor, 53, 66, 69
  internal migration
    in-migration fields, 70
  Migrant and Seasonal Farm Workers Association, 93
  NC Growers Association, 93
  Orange County, 61, 107

Chapel Hill, 20, 23, 48, 56, 61, 64, 65, 70, 71, 92
physiographic regions
  Coastal Plain, 58, 64
  Mountain, 64
  Piedmont, 20, 58, 64, 66
population Change, 50
Raleigh, 20, 23, 41, 48, 59, 60, 61, 69, 124
Raleigh-Durham Chapel Hill MSA, 23, 69, 124
Research Triangle Park, 18, 23, 27, 69, 110
Triangle, 48, 57, 59, 60, 69, 70, 71, 72, 74, 75, 76, 79, 81, 82, 84, 90, 91, 92, 96, 98, 99, 101, 103, 104, 105, 106, 107, 109, 110, 111, 113, 114, 116, 120
Work First Program, *see* Policy, 117
Policy
  Amnesty, *see* IRCA, 12, 14, 85, 102, 114
  Bracero Program, 13, 27
  Governor Jim Hunt, 47, 60, 62, 117
  H-2A visa, 6, 93, 118, 119
  Hart-Celler Act
    Immigration and Reform Act of 1965, 13, 14
  Hart-Celler Act, 1965, 13, 14
  implications, 117
  IRCA, Immigration Naturalization and Reform Act of 1986, 14, 15, 71, 85, 102, 123
  North Carolina Work First program, 117
  PRWORA, Personal Responsibility and Work Opportunity Reconciliation Act of 1996, 83, 94, 117
  undocumented workers, 13, 14, 26, 62, 66, 79, 106, 107, 108, 115, 117, 118, 119
  USAPATRIOT, Uniting and Strengthening America by Providing Appropriate Tools Required to Intercept and Obstruct Terrorism Act of 2001, 118, 119
  WIA, Workforce Investment Act of 1998, 117
Public Opinion about Immigrants, 63, 64, 65, 118
Recruitment
  formal strategies
    accommodations, 102, 103, 115, 116
Recruitment Strategies
  formal
    Employment Security Commission, 96
    H-2A visa program, 93
    job fairs, 92, 93
    newspapers, 26, 71
    temporary agencies, 26, 74, 91, 97, 102, 115
  informal
    Mexican consulates, 94, 115

raiding, 100, 109, 115
word of mouth, 26, 98, 99, 114
Research Methods, 69
  data analysis, 79
  key informants, 72
  newspaper content analysis, 70, 71, 72, 85, 91, 114, 119
  qualitative corporate interview, 75
Rural areas, 10, 16, 19, 20, 22, 34, 39, 41, 45, 46, 53, 113, 119
Spanish
  ESL, English as a Second Language, 56, 62, 102, 103, 115
  media, 72, 119
    newspapers, 59
    radio, 60, 70, 72, 73, 74, 92, 95, 119
    television, 26, 70, 72, 73, 92
Sunbelt, 20, 21, 22, 23, 29, 38, 123
tiendas, 99, 100
Unemployment, 23, 48
United States
  Census

Regions
  East North Central Division, 42, 43, 44, 45
  South Atlantic
    population change, 35
  South Atlantic Division, 34, 35, 36, 48, 85
  West North Central Division, 42, 43, 44, 45, 46
Census Regions
  Midwest, 33, 38, 39, 42
    population change, 42, 45
  Northeast, 42
  South, 21, 34, 38
    population change, 35
  Sunbelt, 20, 21, 22, 23, 29, 38, 123
  West, 34
Hispanics
  spatial concentration, 33
  spatial distribution, 32
  population change, 34, 40
Work ethic, 25, 28, 79, 82, 83, 84, 97, 99, 104, 106, 113, 114, 115, 117